Contents

Preface — Tanure Ojaide vii

DRY SEASON

    Book I: Sorrows of a Town Crier 1

    Book II: Arrowheads to My Heart 31

RAINY SEASON

    Book III: A Carnival of Looters 55

    Book IV: Ubangiji: The Conscience of Eternity 79

HARMATTAN SEASON

    Book V: A Stroke of Hope 91

HARVEST SEASON

    Book VI: The Parliament of Idiots 137

    Book VII: The Fish Rots from the Head 161

Appreciation

Many thanks to the Publishing Houses, Kraft, Beacon: Advantage and H & M, Pacific Coast Africanist Association, and Malthouse, who gave permissions for excerpts in this work.

Preface

These poems bear testimony to Tayo Olafioye's proclivity to poetry, a life-long interest and pursuit. The selection reflects his prolific nature as he records his feelings and ideas in verse. The poems show a wealth of experience that covers the breadth and depth of his humanity. He is political and shows great concern for the good governance of his native Nigeria. One reads his rage against despoilers of the nation and his heartfelt desire for justice and fairness in the land.

Tayo Olafioye is a very sensitive personality and really cares for people whose lot, he strongly believes, should have been much better if leaders and politicians had been selfless and disciplined. Selected poems from, among others, *A Carnival of Looters* and *The Parliament of Idiots* show a concerned poet who ridicules the political excesses of his people. Looters and idiots, the political leaders are either there by force of arms or elected by the masses (more likely rigged themselves into office against the wishes of the people!) show criminal disregard for the interests of the country and its people. Olafioye is passionate and shows tough love for Nigeria. He is occasionally harsh, but this underscores his intense love for the country.

Tayo Olafioye's poems touch all aspects of humanity. He writes on the family, love, friendship, absence, exile, pain, and hope. He has a flair for humor as in his poems, on his pair of shoes, and pounded yam. He can be lighthearted or serious as the circumstance dictates. He is able to remind one of the past for a clearer perspective of today; in other words, the past heritage has bearing on contemporary life and will inevitably lead to tomorrow, which he wants to be much better than now. Olafioye is at once a satirist, a moralist, and a humanist. He is local and global as shown in poems about his Ikale people and other poems written in his various international travels. He is cosmopolitan and yet fits well into the traditional Yoruba world. He is simple and complex at the same time, a quality that comes out of his experiences.

I want to emphasize the tough life experience that inspired many of Olafioye's poems, especially in *A Stroke of Hope*. He has at least twice come close to death and he writes, in his more recent poetry, with a survivor's spiritual ardor about life. His resilience is remarkable and he possesses sturdy hope that guides his life philosophically.

Good poetry, I believe, should have something to say; and Olafioye's poetry has much to say about culture, society, politics, humanity, life, and himself. He can be private and public in his poetic forays. Above all, he is always warmhearted and reading his poetry is taking lessons on the human condition. He has been writing poetry for over three decades and this selection provides the reader to have a holistic view of his creative output and contribution to modern African poetry beside his friends and colleagues.

Tanure Ojaide
Professor of African-American & African Studies
The University of North Carolina at Charlotte

DRY SEASON

When, philosophically, our
individual and private moral
landscape is patched, bereft
of fertilizing nutrition in the
cathedral of nature.

Book I
Sorrows of a Town Crier

Dedication

To my very dear friend, Professor Prescott Nick Nichols, an activist and "the Conscience of his Time," San Diego State University of California, who died in 1987 when we least expected and were least prepared for it.

Your death confirmed your life's work and importance-irreplaceable. 'Till we meet again, we will never forget you. Separation is our fate, and time, our bind. Adieu, Happy heavenly rest as Death is certainly the reductionist factor of life.

For

Peter Paul Wiplinger
The Austrian National Poet
And
Susan Novak
His Versatile Companion: A Polyglot
Without whom the intellectual visit to Austria
Would not have been possible, 1987

Gratitude

To Jamie Anne Guerina, San Diego; for being the compiler of this work.

African Envoys

Some who live abroad,
especially in official capacities,
say:
They are tired of boredom.
Come home darlings:
you will glow
in agonies.

Vienna, Austria, 1984

Nema Problem

The only ones
not confused
by this world
are the fools,
who do not
look around enough
or care a hoot.
I hope I am not one.
The thought
 of the wolf
frustrates the dog.

Belgrade, Yugoslavia, 1984

Epilogue for Tomorrow

For those of you who live tomorrow, one or two or three centuries hence: our present was a dangerous place to live. Believe what you read of us-those horrendous things we did. We mutilated conscience, murdered truth, enthroned mediocrity, slept with pythons called hypocrisy, sycophancy and ethnocentrism. We were the frontiersmen that made your future/present available. We were close to the earth, rustic in our crudities, academic but uneducated, loud without finesse and the sophistication of thinking. So gullible were we that we made heroes of termites that ate the fences of our economic sustenance. Some leaders stashed away millions in foreign banks, lived high on the juices of corruption, loved and built empires for their mistresses while ordinary people lay dead of economic strangulation. Even for the sheer thievery, some of our people still hailed them. The oppressed are sometimes their own enemies. Could you believe it? These were the realities of ancient/modern Africa, when we signed documents with toes and counted flies as human beings. We practiced permissive political prostitution at the expense of the nation. We would never be well until we truly treat our ills with honesty in all facets of our national lives. If not, we would continue to cut each other's throats for the next century. We practiced orthodox religion which, in turn, negated progressive awareness. It deadened our sensitivity to modernity. Your time might be modern—modern Africa when science means awareness. For our time, we could not invent a needle in our own names. Soldiers ruled us at many intervals because, by nature, we were imperious, imperial and impossible. Self-discipline did not agree with us, neither did cleanliness. Every last Saturday of the month, soldiers forced us to clean ourselves and our environment. That was how bad we were. Finally, we had great writers. I mean our own Tolstoy, Dostoevski, Shakespeare, and so on. They lived and faced the harshness of crudity for your sake. They wrote what they saw. How could I make you see what they went through when conscience was dead? I knew some of them: they taught me. A special treat, you would admit, to know the makers of history in your time. This perhaps is the summary of our state of national il-health on the eve of the 21st Century. Well, I must go now, to prepare for my departure. Tell your children that I did my best so that they could be proud of me. The chameleon has done its dance; it's left to the offsprings to use their feet. Hope your time is better than mine. Say me well to all. Your loving great, great, grandfather,

Tayo

Pyjamas

Experience, experience, experience
the result of human interaction,
can be voltage sometimes.
One sunny day I wore
African shirt and pants,
to cafeteria.
A colleague,
whose gaze found
a strange fancy yelled:
"Eh Tayo, I like your pyjamas."

Pyjamas?
my blood
choked me faint.
A friend or a foe?

"Eh, guy," I said, "Tell me:
is it new style, U.S.A.
To wear pyjamas, cafeteria?"
Silence…and a stare.
"Eh, guy! at home,
your papa wears pyjamas—
market places?"
Silence! and eyes dropped.

"Where lies the bed that suggests
arrival of my nap
at cafeteria?"

What else can one expect,
when Tarzan and Daktari are:
daily treats on television,
the major source of misinformation?

To be black at times:
the agony of ages,
I will not accept,
I will never forget.

*University of California
San Diego, 1971*

7

Harmattan Christmas

The earth is harsh
we are hungry,
yet again it's Christmas
time to renew the spirit
We shall endure calmly
for we have the best of gifts
the Christmas mode
of peace, love, hope;
food
for one of our hungers.

The time is harsh
but look at yourself,
look at the beggar,
or the homeless
Who should complain?

The harsh sun,
the harmattan sun,
the Christmas sun,
rises palely,
who can tell
How it will set?

The earth is harsh
we are filled with longing;
again it's Christmas
and the spirit is renewed.
We shall endure quietly
for we have the best of gifts
the Christmas mode
of peace, love, hope;
food for man's hunger
the time is harsh.

Commissioned by NTA Ilorin for their
Christmas Celebration, 1984

Goodbye Mrs. B.H.O. Toye

Thunder
hits us with
the brevity of goodness
what the earth gives
it takes.
What Providence loves
it claims.
We protest since pain
is a reminder.
Wailing fills the chambers of hearts;
embers suffocate our breath.
Oh, Mother earth!
Your goodness
shall sustain our constancy;
past memories
shape our future realities.
We bid farewell;
the second birth
of yourself
beyond our sufferings.

Faate, Ilorin, 1984

Impermanence

I love the changelessness of change,
the consistancy of inconsistancy
and the inconsistency of constancy.
Because they hold true
to their names,
as allies of human species.
Let's then give credit
where it's due.
Caesar's unto Caesar
the knife away from the neck
where it does not belong.

Cork, Ireland, 1982

Existence

Existence makes no sense:
am I supposed
to be grateful
for all the pains of living,
for a creation
not of my asking,
a time table
Not of my making?

I would be better off
as air or mountain—
or as time itself
that has no end
but witnesses all ends,
I would not mind.

I cannot even protest
by killing myself
and so ask time
to leave me alone.
Anywhere we turn
he limits us.
There is no escape,
from his tyranny.

Paris, 1983

Lubokun Spirit
A Sacrificial Chant

Crown prince:
the spirit of Lubokun
attend us today.
The Earth is never sick, so
ward off approaching ills,
a dog never exposes its puppies
to be prey of the wolf.
Shield us from cyclones of life
make perfect our sacrifice.

Igbotako, Okitipupa, 1984

Siblings' Incorrigibility

How difficult it is
to teach a people,
adamant and knowledgeable
only in idiocy.
Guided by the arrogance of ignorance
or limitation,
they scoffed
at the University of life;
and betray
guidance from
its tested results.
Alternatives they chose
swept them back to where
they began,
they persist
hewing water
out of stones,
digging channels
where the ocean dries,
dancing after the drumming stops,
using the 14th
to knock at the door
of the 21st century.

Casablanca, Morocco, 1981

University

Like Plato's Republic, absolute Perfection.
Cannot be, will never be.
The University, a paradox of ideals
where few emerge finished products,
others: half-baked, half-boiled, half-cooked
a miniature state of all and sundry.
Some see white
they call it black,
remaining color-confused permanently,
for electoral ethics
they mirror the state,
once maligned
with missiles of untruths—
chameleons all.
Leaders of tomorrow, Now:
diarrhea of the mouth
allies of mischief.
Academic conceits now their game
in every vice always the elite,
these tunnels without vision.

Lagos, Nigeria 1965

Letter Box

Coming from class daily in the U.S. of A.
I peep afar at metallic squares.
If lid opened laughing—
tickled I am, certain of missives
but if it closed frowning;
frenzied I am, knowing it's empty.
Phew!—Wait a minute Mister,
fastidious human failing!
Why blame a box, for letters
it did not write?
Man's frustration,
against non-speaking things.

La Jolla, California, 1982

The Youth of Kosovo

How lucky you are
when centuries of tomorrow
are fused into years
for you.
Like Pristina
you possess a vitality
that makes you
the rocks of Yugoslavia.
You will never know
War,
say amen.
you will not know
Want,
say amen.
You will never see
Ruin,
say amen.
You will not feel
Death,
say amen.
With elders you have
who needs Lebanon?
Who craves Beirut?
Be hot with love,
be drunk with hope,
be friends with books,
be nice with grace,
be humble with thanks,
on Marshall Tito's Square,
every six o' clock.

Pristina, Yugoslavia, 1984

The Workshop Of Madness

What do you call:
a home without peace,
a father, the drunken sponge,
a mother, the roving eye,
a son without sun,
a daughter without home,
a youth without hope,
a nation without Caesar,
a people without past,
a mind without thought,
a race without soul,
a life without aim/purpose?
The workshop of madness.

Rome, 1986

Maitatsine

God's eyes must be
teary today
for Maitatsines's many comings
God's eyes must be red today,
for what his name has done.
Man's consummate bestiality
to think that we can
spread love through hate.
Felling with ferocity
the trees of life
in this forest of creation.
Love breeds consent
not grind water out of stones
which sparks fires of carnage
in the name of Religion.

Thousands: Innocent heads
left sprawling on the streets
with a million flies feasting
on their necks slit open with knives.

Oh! This Holy Shit!
Nigeria:
my heart bleeds
for the agonies of living
on the eve of the 21st Century.

Vatican, 1986

Wedding Ring

Marriage is in the heart
not in the rings.
In Europe, Africa and America,
Hymen-hunters.
I shudder to say:
Marry
ONE
WIFE
EACH
According to…
but have I not seen many
recast polygamists or born-again bachelors
with no ring to tell.

For you my love
I will wear this ring
in my heart to marinate for you.

Hotel Grande, Skopje, Macedonia

Solape

The painful joy
is to be a parent
especially in distant
circumstance.
You sprout unraveling
the mystery of womanhood.
Each time we meet
my heart visits your morrow
as each parting stabs
my living-death,
as your father.
All that I wish
is the most of life for you,
the Heavens must allow.
Nothing is more precious
than one's only eye.
I can only prepare you
but not win
the challenges of life for you.
The chameleon has taught
its child, all that
is left is to check original
your brothers will come
and the sisters, too.
Take care, if death
deprives you of me.

Skopije, Macedonia, 1986

Pounded Yam

I *am* Iyan, the pounded yam
the successful cultural staple
not your city failure.
I am the beginning and end
of Cultural Festivals.
Without me
no festival is worthy and homey.
Welcome me to your homes
with Efo* and Egusi** soup
to slide me down
the smooth path of the esophagus.
Thank me profusely
for I will bring you deep sleep
to remold your weary bones.
Locate me a cry-baby
and I will teach him
how to give you peace.
The palm wine is an ally,
it adds yeast
to your drowsy eyes
and a healthy
Belch
from the deep of the tummy.

Tarry not:
call me and I will answer
my service is your happiness.

*vegetable
**melon

Merete Torp

Discuss me
only with your heart

You Nordic exquisite
talent in the profile of beauty.

You taught me
the Haiku of words

I taught you
the Haiku of love

In which we found
the gems in our beings.

Together in the noise of silence
we communicate
the Excellence of Emotion.

Adieu Merete
you will never be history
in my memory.

Hotel Europa, Sarajevo, 1986

Merete Talks To Tayo

I feel crazy
I do not know
how to enjoy joy,
because I really like you,
and that is no lie;
you make me laugh always.
Those who know, say:
I never did before in Denmark.
You are fire to my Soul.
I hope it glows
like the sun's eternity,
liking is the mother of Love

Writer's Union Office,
Sarajevo, 1986

Ant

The little tiny one
if a woman were
to have your waist
in ratio to human size
how pretty and
very shapely, we say.
Sweet as she looks
moving as she moves.
But above all
is your brain;
the homestead of order
computer in organization.
You queue and file
in everything,
no matter how long
the journey of pursuit
if only we care
build, queue and file
like you do
Nigeria will be a haven.

Sophia, Bulgaria, September 1984

The Aafin and Ooni Tussle

I wish I know
why the Yorubas
are not grateful
to peace.
Perhaps Afonja's curse
of ingratitude stays.
Fires always flare
in their barns,
storms always rage
in their seas.
Daily festivals of war!
Of late
the two supreme monarchs
deities at large
Deputies of the Supreme
On Earth,
at each other's throat
each claiming to be first.
Their social engineers
perverting the process.
If fathers are airheads
What are the sons and daughters?
Just before this latest
was another tussle
Awo and Akins;
the family became gentiles
and Jews in Egypt.
The forest struck ablaze
from their intransigence
for they failed the warning
in Ogunde's dirge.
All the tortoise
hold the reins on the horse
and are far gone
nor will they yield.
The hare dangles on the scaffold
becoming fodders
for the cattle to feed.

New York, in the air, Swissair No. 426, August 1984

25

Letter to My Kitchen Knife

What do you say
to a friend
who never disappoints—
shine or high waters?
For ten years-
No strike, no vacation,
always responsive
to the banquets of gourmet,
or the signals:
of the earthquakes of the stomach.
Take this poem,
my bouquet of gratitude.
Wish so were man's loyalty
to friends, work and peace,
our happiness would be eternal.

Douvbronik, Adriatic Coast,
August 1984

Marital Infidelity

When trouble is asleep
rather so soundly,
you must do
all possible,
never to wake it up.

Vienna, Austria, 1986

The Liar

A liar's lips
never show blood.

A eunuch's children
are never near by.

Rome, Italy, 1986

American Satire

Stmt...The polls show Americans still support the president despite the latest scandal in Washington.

Trans...No one wants to admit that they voted an idiot into the White House.

Stmt...Donations continue to pour in to the reverend to keep God from calling him home.

Trans...There is a sucker born every minute.

Stmt...The general denied that defects in the Army's new tank could be lethal to our soldiers.

Trans...So what? He doesn't have to ride in it.

Stmt...The college president said the fee increase was needed to maintain academic excellence.

Trans...The new condo was more expensive than he thought.

Stmt...The minister strongly denied that he had a number of moral transgressions with a prostitute.

Trans...Twice in the choir loft, three times in a motel room, and once on the dinner table.

Stmt...The press secretary denied that the president fell asleep during the summit meeting.

Trans...The old buzzard snored like a chainsaw.

Stmt...18 students died during a spring-break riot in Fort Lauderdale.

Trans...Who cares?

Stmt...The official said that revenue enhancement is only attainable through inverse deduction of deficit finance.

Trans...None possible.

Stmt...The pop group Jefferson Starship relaxed today after their last sell-out performance.

Trans...We milked the city for lots of dough.

Stmt...I'm working at DOW Chemical, dad, to help you, the farm, and humanity in general.

Trans...Screw the farm, screw humanity and screw you. I'm in it for the money.

Stmt...Heavy fighting was reported in the Middle East again today.

Trans...What else is new?

Stmt...Oliver North denied breaking any laws during his job at the National Security Agency.

Trans...He's guilty. Guilty, guilty, guilty!

BOOK II
Arrowheads to My Heart

Gratitude

To Tanure Ojaide, University of North Carolina at Charlotte: Africa's Poet Laureate for his review of this work.

To Dooreen Wu of Hong Kong, a scholar with an eagle's eye to pick a needle in a haystack.

Monument to Madness

All Hail
The ignoble
Houphouet Boigny!
His Temple of God
our glorious poverty
at Yamoussoukro
this Basilica in the 'bush'
monument to infamy
another Taj Mahal
at the altar of our insanity
where our emptiness is maintained
two hundred million have nots.

A land:
two hundred million poverties
and God: already—
too many houses over rich.
And why this largest costliest
in Africa: the mystery our madness
history's home of histrionics.
One man's monument
to Self and Infamy.

All Birds do sing
but when It is the Owl
they say it is the witch crying.

Oh Africa:
make not Notoriety our name
this Foolishness my great sorrow
are we better Communicants
Or our prayers more sugary?

Every corner our pains of need
even our souls
are termites disgorged.

Lake Geneva, Switzerland

Brain-drain in Africa

The Labourer tills the sun
    The Harvester sleeps in the shade
Cranks milk the cow
    Commoners lick the crumbs
The truth dies
    Sycophancy its Heir
sheep in death's clothing
    Lead lions in sheep's skin
Ignorance reigns
    Knowledge the bus boy
    Crudity is king
Finesse is criminal
    Tradition stifles
Innovation a bastard
    Religion an opium
Freedom an asthma
    Human rights a myth
Nepotism an ally
    Nationhood a mirage
Tribalism the staple diet
    Minimum essentials
Become Rare commodities
    Collective focus
Not a Value cherished
    Tradition-bound
Emasculates the progress-bound
    13th century
Sneers at the 21st
    Contracts on your head
Signal Boss Protégé promotion
    Clique –Ness is politics
Drowning Progressive principles
    Justice a threat
Appeasement a deal
    We are still dancing, while
Others are on the moon
    Happy crude fools
All about Nothing.

We tolerate our ills too well
    Buffoons that we are
Others would have Seen Red.

Only so much pain and stress
Human Psyche can take
Those with imagination
And its wings will fly
Home is where comfort and happiness abound
Soothing your Broken Heart
The Rest-Only matters of emotion
Arrowheads to my heart.

Rio de Janeiro, Brazil

Feminine Mystique

A woman:
is like a Tea bag.
You never know
how powerful she is
Until…
She is in hot water.
it is Death therefore
that makes the fish
to coil in a static position
not that it could not swim.

Hollywood, USA

My Husband Has Gone Crazy

So my wife fumes
in our daily squabbles
her way of being jolly, really.
We are opposites to each other
as we are of other people, curiously
one is fire, the other water
tension, though mild, is our friend
and the kit of survival.
No spark, no spice—funnyingly.

Her Majesty despises the noise of silence
volcano must be gathering steam
till the next nuclear fuse again.

Curiously: When I am away
I miss the seismic tremor
of her presence.
I must truly be crazy
To wish peace adieu
in my temporary respite.

Lake Geneva, Switzerland

When Daddy Was Away

"Daddy"
"Yes, my darling"
"Don't you
Live with us any more?"
I live with you everyday
in my heart and in my being.
At the age of three
Understand:
I'm one hour away
from you and mommy.
I return home every Thursday
to be with you two
for the weekends
and all holidays.
Ah, yes
I live with you in my being
which is the inner being
of my being.
I live with you all my life
before you were born and thereafter
I live with you
In my sleep and in my dreams.
Oh! Yes, my joyful pain
I live with you in the fullness
of my life which is no fulfillment
without you, my mischievous innocence.
I talk with you at every sunset
before night closes your eyes.
Daddy must provide food
that fuels your health
Daddy must buy clothes
that cover your back
Daddy must find shoes
that warm your feet
Daddy must fetch the fees
that furnish your mind.
Daddy cannot guarantee life
but must ensure your preparedness
Daddy must go where the means
assure your comfort and decency.

"Daddy,
Don't you live with us any more?"
Please, don't say that again
it thunders the chambers of my heart
I miss you too, kiddo.
Heavens hold you gracefully
Will see you very soon
this week, assuredly.

Pasadena, California, USA

Who Am I?

My stereo is Japanese
My car is American
My suit is European
My shoe is Italian
My hair is Angelino
But my heart is African.

Assorted vegetables
Often do agree
In the same pot of soup.

London, England.

Siblings

Most relatives—
Are like the hairs
Of the rear-end,
They will not scrape.
They remain permanent
Nuisance, irritation and itchiness.

Lagos, Nigeria

The Institute of Rumors

There they sew
Not garments of wear
But tales stench-Imagined!
They weave and weave yarns
Expertly computed
Never before known
Only Spiders of Brazil
And Swiss factories compare.

You wonder their Faculties
The types of manure
Sulfurous sepulchers.

Heaven must be red
Victims galore
Of their angular tongues of ice
Amours, events that never were
Not even broached
Their Parrot eyes
Claimed to see
Beyond every reality imagined.

Kisses, visits and talks
Myths of concerns
Mirrors of their own worms.

Stadium Road, Ilorin, Nigeria

The Green Snakes

What some Friends can be!
Don't comeback again
The oil of mask
Cries not only sorrows
But Grudges against your miens.

Noise can never
Kill a tree
That grows
In the marketplace.

San Diego Zoo, San Diego
California, USA

Iyasere

He who lacks regard
let him touch the tail of the lion
that stealthy prowl
is no cowardice of the tiger
but your Solomonic ways to share.

We never met before
perhaps of course,
in the cadence of our songs
echoes in the boulevards of the mind
where we sent ideas, fitted
with the shirts of our moods
shoes of our pains
caps of our thoughts
mutual messages of patriotism
delivered for the past 20 years.

Now face to face
on Lake Arrowhead San
Bernardino Mountains
twenty thousand miles
away from home.
I feel your warmth in my lungs
your Songs in my being
your transparence so encompassing
true to feel noble heritage we knew
so magical to be with you
on this island in the sky.

You will never mud
say Amen
you will never stale
say Amen

You will never skunk
say Amen
with mountains already scaled
eon is your name
Colossal: your size
we must soldier on-
undaunted.

We can live only our time
not the tomorrow
so unknown and elusive
the present is dangerous enough
to breathe.

Room 33, Oak House,
Lake Arrowhead, California, USA

Rienhartsen's Abduction

Only last night
In the world of miracles
Lee Rienhartsen
Six foot plus
Was abducted
By six virgin aliens
What a gag!
In these days of Hollywood.

Pasadena, California

Oh Harry

Oh Harry
The apple to millions
A farmer
Who never abandons
His crops
Because weeds have taken over.
You are the Olumo.*
On which we crest our woes
We know the good *one*
On the day it rains.
You are the mint of Happiness
Yours will be so everlasting.
Your burg, castle and yam
Won't be small but bountiful
Forever colossal and Indian
The *honey pot* of continents.

La Jolla, California, USA

---

*A huge, steady rock in Abeokuta, Ogun State of Nigeria. The Egba
people, who are indigenes of Abeokuta, use the OLUMO rock as their
cultural image of solidarity, strength and reliability.

Teju Ladipo

Africa burns its forests.
Time stopped at your passing
Something so difficult
To couch in words—
My brother-in-law
Engineer under thirty
The best and lone star.
There was no death in your eyes
But in your destiny
In the afternoon of your life
In fact: of our lives.

Each time I see your face
In the memory of yesterday
My heart sinks
Into the abyss of incredulity
We die daily for your loss
The tendril of a palm
The baobab tree of the clan.

Culture and urbanity.
You were the phantom, the mirage
The substance of a broken dream
On the boulevard to prominence
You did not die alone.

Foyin: your niece will never
Know you but only in history
She was a week old when you left
Your imperfections would in others
Have been passport to ancestorland
Yet fate is dictator.
The unfairness of the burden

And the emptiness of life
Much good had suffered ruin
Before the earth destroys evil
Justice is like the moon
Slowly is its gait
Yet covers the earth before dawn.

Adios Teju:
You will be forever warm
In our Hearts.

Vienna, Austria

Memorial Ode to
Mrs. Lucy Aiyedun

Never before has one life been so tried
The travails of this sojourn
Peace not so peacy
Home and its Flowers of Spring
So denied
The Milestones of culture's fulfillments.
Only Fate Understands.

Now She is gone
To the best hallelujah
Of Herself
Here below we celebrate
Your fortitude, talent
And Ebony shines which
On our pains are so etched.

We lose You
But You are home at last
To the Harvest of your niceties
Adieu Mrs. Lucy Aiyedun
We will never forget you

And of course…
Only God knows best.

Ilorin, Nigeria

United Nations of Oratory

On the bridal night
The groom became
A clawless lion
Howling passion without grit.
United Nations without teeth
Each veiled in conceit
Of inaction to stem the human sacrifice
To grudge and discontent.
Words: their Masks
Yugo's geography: their excuses.

The moon must not discriminate
It shines for all: The good and the bad.
Elders must take blame
For not behaving their age.
If the community under their nose
Lapses into anarchy
300 years of civilization
Have come to nought.

Geneva, Switzerland

The American-cut Penis

Only in America!
The Ecuadorian housewife
Yanked the hubby's phallus
With the butcher's special knife
Trophy for the rapist Nero.

Messages for all males
This mark of War

Nightly stupors of the bouncer
Triggered libidinous visits of violence. Imagine her pain
Perhaps, audacity: the rascal
Yanked the beef out of the window
For the fowls to peck.

Messages for all males
This mark of War

Imagine again
His sputtering all over the floor
As he dashes from
Pillar to pillory
Hollering unimaginable agonies
Red water Gushing the main pipe
Death knocking at the door?

Messages for all men
This mark of War

Imagine the police
Picking up the loot of iniquity
The Doctors' nine hours
Labour attachment

Messages for all males
This mark of War
Rape:
A Woman's psychological doom.
The yank:
Man' certificate of Death—
A universal disgrace.

Santa Rosa, California, USA

The Rite of Passage
Dr. Clyde St. Hill
The Okonkwo of Barbados

Well, my friend, now you know:
Life is Empty
It is like a flicker-
A micro-dot in Eternity.
We will always miss you. Goodbye till we meet again.
And to you:

O'dua, my ancestor, bring back my friend
Tomorrow is too late
His battered heart now a stone.
The baobab tree has fallen
The elephant can no longer stand on its hinds.
You have fueled poison into my bones
And I am not grateful.
Tears are still standing
On my pillow.

San Diego, California, USA

Rainy Season

When the national weather was inclement, sustaining a deluging typhoon of moral pollutions. When we stared cinematically, at the bloody albums of time and intractable insufficiencies, brought about by uncircumcised mammons and uniformed, home-bred godzillas with hairs between teeth. Even our women refrigerated cocaine in their honey-pots and brought home HIV's from abroad as their modern golden fleece of death. It rained and poured—jolly well. Almost a fifth of the populace infected. Native mediciners lied with confidence that betrayed home cure, in order to stack their vaults with death-money which fought biology with ineffectiveness.

BOOK III
A Carnival of Looters

Introduction

When will this Carnival for Looters End?
Notes on Tayo Olafioye's *A Carnival of Looters*

This is a major publication of a book of poetry that Tayo Olafioye has put out in this country, the place of his birth. He currently stays and teaches in San Diego, California, where he is a distinguished professor of literature. This publication marks a major turn in his poetic career since he emigrated to the United States in the late 1980s. The reason for this movement into the world where he is not culturally anchored is a painful one, yet the inevitability of the choice is even more painful to this poet whose lines reek of painful memories of the geography of home. This is the crux of this book of poems. In it, Olafioye dialogues with his native society, those he has left behind, his beleaguered country, creating a pattern of remembering, which is littered with anger and hope on the one hand and on the other hand, a sense of pity for those who engage in the wanton plunder of his homeland, his county, Nigeria. That he loves his country is not in doubt at all. The fact that he insists that this volume of poems must be published here in Nigeria bears a curious testimony to that irreducible fact. He loves his country with the anger of someone who cares for its health. As the celebrated African-American writer, James Baldwin, once remarked, to love one's country is to be critical about its hateful history, its unwholeness, its idiocies. In this sense, loving and hating are not polar regimes of living, rather they exist to check and maintain a balance in man's very existence. This balance is very necessary in every society. This is what Olafioye seeks here.

Like patriots all over the world, what Olafioye strives for is to create, at least in his poetry, this balance by insisting upon making obvious the imbalance of contemporary Nigeria's social existence. In this sense, Olafioye suffers the fate that all poets must carry in similar social and political contexts. This is the kind of poetry that comes from the deep recesses of a heart tortured by deeds which belittle and denigrate humanity. It is this kind of poetry which Pablo Neruda describes as imperfect:

> A poetry impure as the clothing we wear, or our bodies, soup stained, soiled with our shameful behavior, our wrinkles and vigils and dreams, observations and prophecies, declarations of loathing and love, idylls and beasts, the shock of encounter, political loyalties, denials and doubts, information and taxes ("Toward An Impure Poetry," 1994).

Tayo Olafioye's poetry is all of this. It is political. It is cultural and beyond all of this, it is an inner quest to conquer the turbulence of his world. And because it is all of this, Olafioye insists on making this voice public first in his own country, this crucible of the new morbid face of post-colonial conditions.

This volume then is an important contribution to that kind of poetry written "at certain hours of the day and night to look closely at the world of object at rest" (Neruda, 1974), the mark of which is the harsh revelation of life in its starkest form. The tone of *Carnival of Looters* is harsh in part, quick and witty, and the tempo is vibrant, topical. The anguish expressed is lyrical, properly laced with elaborate satirical bites. This is a very significant feeling that the reader experiences as he reads through the line of Olafioye's lyrical anguish which is an intervention of Nigeria's narrative idiocies.

The first part of the collection, "Another Spring of Meaning" explores the poet as a father tutored by the tenderness of care and loving. This section has a total of three poems, "Treasures," "To my daughter Anna" and "Orion." The first is written by the poet's six-year old daughter and the other two by his students at the University where he teaches. The inclusion of these poems here is meaningful in more ways than one: it is a direct declaration of the poet's tenderness towards the humanity around him. In a very important way, "To my daughter Anna" can be parachuted into the larger engagement of *A Carnival of Looters*, which is the undying love for one's country. In this sense, Anna becomes the symbol of a country for which the poet (mother) tames sleepless nights in order to understand. The second part, "The vision of Crazy Looters" best exemplifies the closeness of this poet's definition of poetry to the "ordinary" touch and feelings of living, unornamented real.

"My patriotic quest" is significant in many ways as it foregrounds the debate of nationhood and nationality in a plural society on the verge of disintegration. Central to the debate generated in this poem is "the need to question and relocate the nation in this turbulent times" as the saying goes here. The answer which the poet proffers lies in the nostalgic response to and longing for the comfort provided by the discourse of ancestral world. This theme of nationhood and the question which it has generated in post-war, post oil-boom Nigeria has been in common decimal in recent Nigerian art, especially in recent poetry and novels. It has also found persuasive expression in recent scholarly writing. The whole gamut of Tanure Ojaide's poetry from *Children of Iroki and Other Poems*, (Greenfield Press, 1973) to his latest collection of poems, *Delta Blues* and *Home Songs* (Kraft Books, Ibadan, 1998) is replete with this theme. Wole Soyinka's *Open A Continent: A Personal Narrative of the Nigerian Crisis* (Oxford University Press, 1996) is to date the most eloquent testimony of the many shades in this debate. In the first chapter of this polemical book, Soyinka poses and reposes this question: "when is a nation?" with the ultimate intention of eliciting critical responses from the reader to the idea of nation (and subject). In other words, Soyinka is asking: when does a subject acknowledge a nation as his? Soyinka only hints at the possible answer, he does not give an absolute one.

Olafioye's poetry asks this question outside the vision of the rulers which he refers to as "the looter." It is a critical question only patriots ask. This is why "The pathology of hope" rejects the "vacant notion of nation building" since "Death has no assignment/in a deserted home."

In Olafioye's poetry, the conceptual difficulty of the question, "when is a nation," is not left float aimlessly in its intellectual orbit. It is concretized by the poet's reduction of its essence to bare human existence. The whole ideal is concretely redeemed in the poem "Martyrdom." This poem extols the worth of Ken Saro-Wiwa, the Ogoni Environmentalist and Civil Rights activist hanged on November 10 by the Abacha Regime. Here is how the shock of Ken Saro-Wiwa's death is recorded:

> In you Ken lived the muse:
> language lost one of its alphabets
> that dead day in our November.

Ken Saro-Wiwa is a symbol of the dissenting majority of Nigerians. He is the embodiment of the question: "when is a nation?"

Never tired of restating the obvious, "Mission abroad" reposes the questions: "how do we carve a new nation?," "when is a nation?" The answer provided by the poet is not surprising: "Poetry must whittle new alternatives."

Nationhood and citizenship (subject) debate is only one of Olafioye's concerns in this collection, although it is an overriding one. He writes about love, too. This is the longing for a glorious past that was lately submerged in a carnival of shameful deeds in this kingdom of looter.

How else can I end this brief and probably unfinished remarks on the poetry of this distinguished professor of literature but to go back to his poetic manifesto:

> We must use poetry for politics
> Or politics of poetry,
> Our nuclear bombs of the mind.

For now this is the only reassuring space for poets. After all, Olafioye confides in us:

> We are all patients
> In the hospital of guilt,
> Dancing together in sadness.
> I know this because I live it.

And for posterity, the only hope of redemption, Olafioye has this terse verse:

Be still in your soul,
My child.
Daddy did not stand at roadside
Like a tree askance.
His pen wept his time
And sang its happiness.

I find reading Olafioye's book of poems a rewarding experience for many reasons, one of which is that it restates, in concrete terms, the blinding realities of Nigeria's post-independence social and political madness.

Onookome Okome
University of Calabar, Nigeria

My Patriotic Quest

Silence is the graveyard of hope.
But…
how do you ask ancestors
why the country we love
now sour and a firestorm—
sandunes suffocating the sea?

How do you ask ancestors
why born a nation
that rows backwards in
the boat of progress?

How do you write your pains
in words of comfort
for the hungry and dying?
Tribal phantoms of social lepers.

How do you sing a people—
demoralized and broken,
breathing fiery droughts
in their nostrils?

How do you pray for hope:
a nation
ruled by demons
With hairs between teeth?

Implode: crisis of mind
Expunge: politics of grief
Advance: sacrifice of peace.
Nothing happens by itself.

Abhor masquerades of charades,
stare honesty in the gut.
This, Aiyekoto-the parrot, says,
Nigeria's only road to resurrection.

The Pathology of Hope

We stagger,
disaster to disaster,
blind to the better self.
Only the parasites cheer
in the festival of loot.

We indulge
the pathology of hope:
that God exists;
that God will judge;
that God will save.

Unwilling to pay the price;
to save ourselves;
to save the nation.
ours: the pathology of hope;
ours: the pathology of myths
managing the misery
of human condition,
no matter the evil;
we must "manage."

But manage what?
corruption:
hopelessness?
Helplessness?
Poverty of the soul;
ineffectual tolerances
self-defeating appeasements;
a vacant notion of nation-building;
failure and self-condemnation.
Death has no assignment
in a deserted home.
When ancestors lived,
masquerades balanced
masks backed assistance
of illiterate guns.

Martyrdom

Many a thing:
fitting a noble;
not knife to the heart of man;
even tirades of words and intrigue.

Whatever the cause…
many
victims go beyond this world:
Lumumba went that way;
Yitzak Rabin;
Ken Saro-Wiwa…

The world soon forgets,
but not the stones left after the storm,
the pain, a nail-sore,
even if life marches on.
A life is still a life;
better not wasted.
The body is usually affected
when the head is brutalized.

In you Ken lived the muse:
language lost one of its alphabets
that dead day in our November.
Your imperfections now their perfections.

Whatever veneer of dignity you summoned
is now transparent lowliness.
More than silver, we lose,
the cosmetics yielding, finally,
to our crudity.
no place to hide;
the dyke is broken.

Easy to own a God;
hard to keep rules—
rules of the day:
the jungle of Serengeti.
Untie the paranoia, Mr. Military…
and you, a cattle-egret,
will be without delay.

Ogoni People

Betrayals embrace your beings,
as you wear the garments of thorns.

Tiny in number;
mighty in spirit;
elephantine
shore to shore.
A hero dies
fame is put aflame.
The world
claims you.

Cheated for eons;
embraced for life.
You: the rocks;
we: the termites.
You: of David;
we: the swines.

Without your gold,
the Niger flow—
a desert of lizards would be.
You: the grass;
we: the machetes.
Is this the price to pay?

Your inheritance to maintain.
the world knows, they must avenge.

You: the parable; rich little girl;
hidding in the bush from the Big Foot.
Yours: the golden heart.
Theirs: the stench of miens.
Only death removes the bitterness
of a blinded people.

Missions Abroad

Consulates of stench;
their master's voice;
defenders of hell;
cymbals of ignominy;
agents of Nero;
egregious maggots of state;
eclipse of African genius;
incubus at large;
sons and daughters of January;
farmers of crops of deceit;
engineers of misinformation;
architects of retrogression;
doctors of lunacy;
professors of vacancy;
editors of misology;
Christians without Christ;
Muslims without Mohammed
ambassadors of bashing;
Soyinka, their dog;
lawyers of liars;
flocks without shepherd;
nation without Mandela.

How do we carve a new nation?
poetry must whittle new alternatives—
just a simple cathedral or mosque
of honesty, fairness and justice.
Not the magisterial grandeur of emptiness
nor the anthills of moral invalids.
This is the meaning—
honesty, decency, conscience, honor—
our government of world acclaim.

Then will come the peace
and respect.

Great Nations or Otherwise

Great nations:
> Books of their deeds;
Great nations:
> Books of their words;
Great nations:
> Books of their visions;
Petty nations:
> Books of their stench;
Batty nations:
> Works of their shame;
Ratty nations:
> Poems of their tricks;
Rigid nation:
> Sounds of their farts.

So does Nigeria today:
Not in Character
To practice the truth.
Even an Oreo cookie
Harbours sugar and calico
In its elements.

Pathological Intellectuals

Hypnotic limitations
tied us to the altar
of collective misery
and total shut-out.
Jolly good sissies;
twenty years behind
the professional troupe.
Only magic reams of – "to appears".
Not the thoroughbred
for nation-building and
harmony of the tongues.

Aggravations,
rumors,
falsehoods;
dog-eat-dog
ego massage.
No substance to life;
menu of academic vacuity
dodos in doldrums;
arrested development syndromes;
carnage of education:
our only resource.
What future, though?
Oh, debilitating society;
the palm-tree that hates the gourds
should not produce wine.

The Bloody Album of Time

The dead have no opinion.
Even if they do,
No one ever believes
Or cares to follow.
But art is immortal,
Recording:
Time, Deeds, and Judgments.
So we may never forget.

Trust not the authors of death,
They deface history
Or bury, with no whims,
If so allowed.
Only Art: the immortal,
The eyewitness.

See Bosnia, the Middle East, Iraq and
Chechnya and Sierra Leone.
Nothing differs from before,
Unless Churchill eluded you
And the burning city of Dresden.
The bard wonders
If we ever learn a thing from
The bloody albums of Time.

Africa and Europe

Africa: the crisis
Of European mind:
Too hot to handle.
Something romantic
About pristine origins,
Not when a permanent
Way of life, or
The savage state
Of human condition.
However,
We are the humans
They had little way to be
The distant cousins
They could not convert:
Too hot to tame.

They chose to abandon us
To the hapless state.
We resisted efforts
To clone us
Their world view:
Too hot to touch.

You can only walk around
The pepper plant;
Climb it: your peril.
The defiance of Africa: a mystical logic.

How Long: Africa?

Africa:
How many years more
To take the forward step?
Ankles still chained to iron bony.
Many nations, now mighty,
A colonized past recount:
England under Rome;
China under Japan;
France under Germany;
Germany under Allied accord.
How long will it take?

We busy ourselves
Inventing corruption
And toilet humors for modernity.
What happened:
The big claims in history?
Timbuktoo in Mali:
Premier citadel of learning?
Tripoli and the caravans;
Extraordinary surgeries,
Iron-smelting and the rest:
All historical firsts.
Why are our descendants adrift?
Can't build on famous past?

The world awaits your glow.
The golden fleece waylaid by
Cockroaches
Clothed in uniform,
Claiming they carry the flag.
Poor flag!
Sad flag!
Tattered flag!
Tarnished flag!
Unhappy in the wind,
Hoping for the next smile
Of the sun of providence.

Tanure Ojaide: The Gong at Dawn

This name is music
To my tongue,
Defies affiliations,
The geography of distance.
Like his work,
Every place
Is home to the
Majesty of his depth.
Monarch of the Pen, he
Straddles the winds
Of the Universe.

No clime rejects his breeze,
Without which,
No life pulsates the mind.
A mature maize that does not
Shoot off;
A yam tuber that does not
Boast.
The lion that
Moves stealthily
To devour
The most meat.
His Kolanut speaks,
According to the mind
Of a breaker.
Death has no assignment
In his house,
Wherein lives truth with eternity.

The man sits under the tree
To tell how the wind
Blows; more fluid
To your pen,
And balance to your mind.

Bayo Ogunjimi
The River That Never Moved

Not many exits
In this life
Reflect a man and
His environs,
As Bayo Ogunjimi's:
Many fronts—
The river swallowing the sea.
Now he knows:
The woods avenge
Themselves with finality.
No one damaged in
Half-measure.

The physical exhaustions:
Conviction, principle, conflicts,
Contract their yams, pounded—
Wrenchingly.
The sun scorches
Its own forests to dust.

His volcanic eruptions;
Complexity;
Stiff neckedness;
Combativeness;
Scholarliness;
All smith-mold him
From the birth of time.

Against the gods
Nothing seems ordinary.
Fever and kidney:
A two-headed constrictor.
Those gloating needlessly,
Problems remain stubborn
Realities.
Levels of cynicism beyond compare.

Complicated man:
That was his lot.
Minstrel of ditties:

That was his gem.
"Wicked analyst."
That was his style.

A river that never moved
Has flowed its course.
His deed is done.
What is yours?

Monkey in London

Monkey go London kom back,
Na monkey e still be.

Revisional changes,
We need;
From within.
Must have
Zestful embrace
Of life and exposure.

Oscillating like
The pendulum,
Without thorough digest,
Is playing the monkey's
Visit to London.

My Pikin de Waka Skul

Never present in the morn,
When my child
Waka go skul:
An experience so magnetic,
I always missed.

Out of the car she jumps,
Racing like an arrow;
Class-ward,
Not looking back,
Nor care in the world, a mission of scholarship,
Her goal.

What a life?
What passion?
What a love?
Seriousness of purpose,
Innocent and pure,
That touch my being of being.

She who makes an early start,
Will rest at mid-day.
None like a child,
Especially mine.
Not by height,
We know maturity;
Only by deed;
 Blessed her, O atavism! Lubokum,
Tears tailing my cheeks…

Our Uncle: Adieu

(for Chief Olu Akinfosile)

Of what use is a man
Who does not contribute
To his time? But you did.
Your name, Uncle—
Is a song in our tongues.

A mature maize,
    That did not show off.
A baobab tree,
    That did not boast.

Every place was home
To the Majesty of your depth.
The monarch of kindness—
    The weakness of your being,
Even at your own expense.
You were foolishly good
In the land of locusts and bats.

    We shall miss you.

Your life straddled the winds
Of the universe.
No clime rejected your breeze.

Even when the river dries,
    Its name will always remain.
No noise of the market
    Will ever kill your tree…

For Death
    —has no assignment—
    With your name
Wherein lives truth with eternity.
The present is testimony to our untruths.
Your humanism,
Your denied pains.
Your memory shall not lose its rightful place.

We, the Ikales,
    Are the orphans of your hopes.
How should we sing your life
In the words of glory?

Only God knows.
Here, we celebrate it anyway:
In Posterity and Motionless Eternity

    Adieu, God's speed, Uncle.

    We shall never forget you.
    And,
    Angels shall chorus your name.

Ken Saro-Wiwa

Behind the mind of God
Are His eyes that see all things

Your life expired, Ken—
Without completion,
Compliment of the uniform;
A rush to judgment,
A rush to boulevard of
Dubious self-righteousness.

Tribal justice celebrates:
The carnival of gloating;
The hot iron melted;
A relief for the cheetahs.
Some made hefty loots, local and
Foreign minders of our ill-health;
The festival of treachery;
This their apogee of evil.

To the arrogant oligarchy,
Little matters anymore,
Echoes of Saro-Wiwa assail the world.

May his spirit forever torment your sleep
And castrate your manhood
On the bed of ignominy.
He who swallows a needle
Will forever sleep standing up.
Whoever takes fresh garlic
Will forever carry smells in the gut.
Ken, the galaxies worship your name.

BOOK IV
UBANGIJI: The Conscience of Eternity

The Beast* of Songhai

Death, more delicious
than honey on the palate of Evil.
Reason for snacking tuber-seeds
    Of the morrow
in the barnyard of self-preserve.
Many patriot-warriors and prophets
already swell the mounds.
The grave-vaults seep
with the blood of their innocence.
Time will bring them to greenery.
you cannot cover the sun
with your fingers. For,
time unfolds like a paper.
Whoever overeats
must vomit or swell up;
you cannot pitch
without being defiled.
This navigator of ethnic fire-storms
met own flight to perdition
Obangiji* the conscience of eternity
please intervene, perpetually.
The eyes of the world, speak our dirge.
Time unfolds like a sheet of paper,
you were there in Azania
Where our worries died.
Evil has no colour, we know
never before has a home-grown Godzilla
menaced the forests of peace.
    His teeth bled
the hot bloods of death in West Africa.

*Beast: A military Head of State reputed for ignorant brutality.
*Obangiji: Hausa word for God, the Supreme Being. Spelt traditionally as "Ubangiji."

The Pariah Nation

In every vein, flows the germ of corruption
Our leaders long exiled peace
To suffocate hope.
At the foot of the rock — Aso Mines*
At the foot of governance — the tortoise and the fox
At the foot of justice — vultures and rakes
At the foot of technology — incompetent impotence
At the foot fairness — two faces of Janus
At the foot of principle — money and scums
At the foot of the table — hunger and crumbs
At the foot of the nation — dishonour and death
At the foot of trust — betrayal and hate
At the foot of hope — ruins and ruins
At the foot of love — profligates et al.
At the foot of Savannah — locusts and bees
At the foot of the Iroko — termites and snakes
At the foot of the black gold — 419s and putrids
At the foot of the world — pariah and skunks

They Stole Our Voice

I stand by the tree of my feelings
Kneading my damaged in-existence—
The mythical suspension of my being.
I felt the flames of emptiness
And swam
The rivers of endurance.
I have known the blindness of fate
And asked:
Is the moon already out tonight?
For, my mind shines interior darkness.
I have felt the pangs of silent impatience
Waiting for the rains of glee
To shower the land, from Savannah to sea.
Events kept stealing our voice
Many deaths in the wombs of hopelessness
Staggering as weary lions
We refused an early death,
But our troubles still measure infinity.

There is nothing more unfeeling
Than to sleep with uncertainty.

Sometimes

Sometimes I blame fate
Sometimes I flail God
Sometimes I rail genes
Sometimes I blame birth
Sometimes witches and wizards
Sometimes I see race
Sometimes yesterday desired.
Sometimes I crave tomorrow
Sometimes I know nothing
Sometimes I am vain
Sometimes I am a sycophant
Sometimes I am a lie
Sometimes I trust as a child
Sometimes I am fantasy
Sometimes I miss home
Sometimes I ditch faith
Sometimes I say, why me?
Sometimes I am my root—
My weepy father
His non-conformities.
Sometimes I do not know
Who I am.

Fofo

You are my emerald, the golden egg of my eyes—
You were my search
For permanence,
My only translation of existence.
Death too will be forgotten
For ages, you will carry the flag
For fate, too, selects its own society.
Nothing untoward ever
But happiness and growth.
Nature binds you to me
Heart to heart,
Soul to Soul—
Daddy's wish for your dawns:
Hard drive in scholarship
Hard till in industry
Hard work in discipline
Hard on irreverence
Hard going on frivolity
Hard views in life's chores
Soft smiles in diplomacy
Warm touch, a sensitivity
Hot blows to irregularities
Smooth runs for longevity
Luck and all else will stand in line.

My Edenic Violet

I litter the winds with my thoughts
When absence replaces the reality of your presence.
Were my thoughts soldiers
I would've summoned arrest of you
Were my feelings concrete
I would've tied you to their trunks
If my heart had bled sugars
I would've turned them sacraments of devotion
It is not the winds we feel
But the little things you do
To affirm my worth.
Nothing lasts forever
Let's make ours, monument to eternity.
Loneliness waits like a beast
In the rainfalls of sorrow.

For Grandma Dejuola

Grandma:

I am sorry—
My adult-world
Can now see
Your sacrifice and love,
My toad eyes could not.
I am sorry
For the totems
My child memories betrayed
My unconsciousness of stone
Now, a parent myself
I could see your sweat
Glistened in solid golds of service.
Showered us with rainfalls of affection
Always armfolds of happiness
At your door, larger
Than aerodromes combined.
You listened to our tales
Still loved even when the world detracted
Above all:
Shielded us from those glaring parents
Because you were there,
I thank you,
Mother Earth
The rich spring
Of our beginnings.
Sleep in tranquility through our memories.

How I Write

I love the noise of silence
Allows my drafts re-worked
The actual art of the mason.
Let it lay to breathe.

Commonsense of the Deep
Not always as common
As the name suggests.

You have a right to be wrong
So long I suffer no
Mental constipation
When the printer's devil
Assails my craft.

The man who fails to tend his farm
Will wail on the day of harvest
Do not mope at me
Like an Egyptian mummy
When galley enemies
Assail my art.

Rewrite, the actual writing
Lay it aside and let it breathe
Re-visit again and again—

A new freshness, vista and vitality
My gains.

On the Retirement of My Shoe

Thank you my black shoe
These 7 years of service.
Designer holes on the sides
Breathing summer airs to feet.
Now scaly, the sloughs of time.
Leather latches are loose now
Pitiable clasp of old self.
Bucket holes in the soles
Despite many visits to doctors of shoes.
Ample halls of academia
You have plied.
Many calico socks
You have flaired
Albeit, for social mischiefs
In spite of little daughter's frown
On your age
Can I rest you
With the mathematics of nostalgia,
By bountiful memories of gratitude?
Life can be hard and empty
But you make it pleasant
To tread on its face.

Harmattan Season

Is when the dry cold blurry and blustery wind of ill-health hit this chronicler, from north down south corporeally. So incendiary the harmattan, that its conflagration deforests in a flash. After the burn, however, sprouts a new garden of hope, trees and foliage—a mahoganic rejuvenation of the poet. The spiritual universe was watching. To them, the glory and praise. A personal testimonial: death has no assignment-yet-in this writer's home. Fate has turned mourning to dancing for him and his family—at large. He survived, trudging on courageously like a tortoise, the old man of the desert.

BOOK V
A Stroke of Hope

Gratitude

To my students of the past and present, at home or abroad, I am profoundly thankful to have met you. One generation replaces the other. It never grows old. You have brought me oceans of enrichment and honey beyond your years. If circumstance makes it difficult for me to ever see you again, along the way, please understand and remember me, but do not be sorry. Life evokes its own justice and its inevitable conclusions. I have had a jolly good ride. If I survive, we'll live to smile again.

To my friends, who at various stages have contributed to my scholarship, an immense appreciation from my heart. Heaven's Gold Medal of Paradise to Kim Dettrey, Jason Josafat, Lalo Reyes, David Depew, Theresa Santos, Cheryl Jovillar, Peejay the Great, Ivan Avina, Lindsey Wagner, Carlos Crouse, Frank Young, and Katerina Mellos. None of you is an African but you sang to me universal tunes of kindness, care and scholarship. If I ever meet God, I'll tell Him I know you.

Even on one's deathbed, one always breathes the hope of living and planning. For down deep into my innermost being of being, I never entertained death or dying; even remotely. I thought I was a rock. My self-delusion was however, punctured wide open one day, when my younger brother, Dr. Shalewa Olafioye, called to inform me that my eldest child, Solape, had been drenching herself in a rain of tears over me. Many members of our family shared her fears. They saw in me, felt in my voice, and smelt in me, what I did not. Those who were close to my daughter, could not stem her torrents. Suddenly, it hit me, the possibility of it, that I might not make it. Sometimes, illness is a betrayal. The thought of it, that some people so genuinely cared, touched me so intuitively and inmostly. I never knew that my life could be so deeply impact their own. I am truly, very grateful. To all my relatives, young and old, brothers and sisters, you all know how I feel about your inner turmoils and anguish. Life is a preparation for death but my inner thoughts are on survival even though I have nothing but books to bequaeth.

Jumoke Okoya-Olafioye wears the head gear of honor and the heart of a lioness. She is my youngest brother – Tunde Olafioye's wife in London. I have never met her. Despite the rigors of her studies at the University of East London - Masters in Business Information System – she still finds the time to e-mail me or send me a card every week asking after my health; with prayers. That's all she has. How do you refund such a goodness!! Leave it to the galaxy of deities. They see every heart.

---

*Aso Rock: Official residence of the Nigerian president but Aso mine has many levels of interpretation. Corruption, mining their gold or fortune. The loot of the nation is also theirs. Aso-oopopoomineral mines.

Foreword

The biography of my illness

—Tayo Olafioye

This season has been horrible, the weather of my health, inclement. That I live to write about it, is my celebration and therapy. Not often does a writer make public the confessional state of his or her health. The only thing to prove is that, at times, it is possible to survive the collective interventions of expertly care, manifold beatitudes, tailored living, inestimable luck and ancestral fortifications. They refuse to condone any of my bouts with cyclonic daze. Many have succumbed to lesser travails.

Stage I

It started in a week when incontinence visited me; frequent urination, that is. My Yoruba cultural background would probably have dubbed it. "a-to-gbe," an attack of urinary drain. By mid- week, I made it to the hospital for investigation, at the Kaiser Permanente Hospital on Zion in San Diego, California. The doctor demanded a urine specimen which the laboratory analyzed with immediacy.

The doctor, Nathaniel Nitahara, suspected an enlarged prostate. "What is that?" I snapped. "I have never heard of it." "Don't worry," the doctor consoled. "Let's find out first." The nurse motioned me to enter a privacy to disrobe and put on a hospital garment with a split back. I did as ordered. I was led to a theatre adorned with medical gadgets and lights. I was asked to lie on a long table, padded nice and clean with a calico sheet. "The doctor will soon be with you," the assistant offered.

The doctor soon arrived and he introduced his retinue of medical nerds. They spoke soothingly as to calm my frayed nerves. I had no idea what to expect. Every member of the team dressed in green hospital garbs. They wore gloves and half masks to entertain their nostrils and mouths. The doctor told me what to anticipate but I had no practical, or mental inkling of what he meant. I lazily understood him. He proceeded to introduce my behind by yanking it to the cold air with an open space before everyone's prying eyes. I felt violated but who was I to squawk before death? The doctor showed me a thin, long, steel, brassy, stick or baton, supposedly a camera that violated my internal organs. The doctor gently guided it on an investigative tour of my inside from the entry gate of my behind. Suddenly, I heard a click and a sharp bite drinking my blood as its beverage. "Be calm," the doctor consoled. "Seven more bites and we will be through." There is no hidden hand without a hidden fist. The team was watching my inside on the monitor all along. This was the beginning of my ordeals.

Days later, the doctor announced that this tomato size object called prostate was very large and must be removed shortly after a second investigation. If not, it would turn cancerous. It had been pressing on my urinary tract, hence the incontinence.

No sooner than that when I received a call, that the doctor needed me to visit him without delay. "You have a choice," the doctor announced. "You can let the prostate grow bigger and bigger and let it turn deadly cancerous, or we remove it now with some risks." "What risks?" I inquired timidly. The doctor replied, "Well, we cannot guarantee that the lines of your sexual function will remain. Doctors make mistakes. We may not be able to save it."

Some cold shivered down my spine. I have really had it, I thought. "But my wife is still young." I protested. "I understand that" the doctor said endearingly. "It is not definitive that this scenario will play out but we must let you know, just in case. Why don't you think about it and read lots of literature on prostate. Talk to people. Seek other opinions and let me hear from you soon so that we can schedule a date for the surgery. It is very urgent. We may be lucky to arrest a lot of unpleasantness now."

I was bemused, confused and dazed. In one stretch, my life seemed at an end. A storm was gathering before my eyes. There was not telling what devastation it would cause. I concluded that I would lose my family life. This was a living torture, an emotional inferno and mostly a psychological death. I race to a precipitate bonfire of conclusions. It was all over, I professed. What a laughing stock I would become. What a toothless bulldog staking the street!. A stallion without stamina! What a state of psychological vacuity! You want to know that it is there, if you need it or that you are complete even if you do not need the weapon from your arsenal.

I summoned courage to call my old reliables to know more about the disease. "You will be fine," reassured Dr. John Olowoyeye, a cardiologist in northern California. We were contemporaries at the grammar school called, Christ's School, Ado-Ekiti in Western Nigeria.

"I believe in prayers," counseled my cousin, Dr. Oke Ibitoye who practices medicine in Maryland. From his base in Staton Island in New York, another cousin, Dr. Odimayo Akindutire declared, "Nothing is beyond the reach of the Almighty. His long healing hand can reach all nooks and corners. There is no need to panic." Both doctors gave calls to Dr. Nitahara, the surgeon in charge. They made their own inquiries. My little brother, Dr. Shalewa Olafioye, an AIDS expert, was not fazed by my commotion. "Big fellow, I advise that you listen to your doctor. I would love to know more of the history of your condition."

We had the surgery. All the poems about it are the speaking pictures of my experience. I did almost a week in the hospital. Dr. Nitahara, as the head surgeon of my ordeal, made his rounds quite often. He told the family that all went well. My mother-in-law was with us at the time. The doctor intimated that all the offending diseases were removed and stated: "The prostate was gone and no cancer of any type lingers around. We need to monitor you for sometime to come. In addition to everything else, I am happy to inform you that you are a full man. Nothing was cut. Your manly functions remained in tact, you should be pleased to know." I responded, "Yes, I am. Even if I do not use my instrument, it is satisfying to know that it is there. I already felt its movement."

"Yes, it is called an erection, you suffer no erectile dysfunction at all. I noticed that you did not take your pain medicine. You endured those terrible pains. You are a very brave man," said the doctor. "The pains were severe, doctor. I got used to them. So, I held out without medication. I tried to ignore the pain. May be I am crazy," I said.

When a sick person is maturing to a candidacy in expiration, the family practices a cover-up of the nature of illness. If he or she were eminent, society would practice media speculation and denials from spokes-persons. They claim in the lingo of the sophistacted—privacy. The irony is that when the candidate eventually kicks the bucket, the silly cat will jump out of the bag and assume a life of its own. Worse still, traditional societies often swing to wide extremes. They read diabolics into the affliction. Everyone suspects the other in the family as the errant witch or wizard. All nocturnal movements, or proverbial ditties, are placed under the umbrella of suspicion. The head co-wife, in a polygamous setting, becomes hunted by the husband's relatives. So also is any of the other wives. An innocent or bitter relative, distant or near, could be in jeopardy. Family quarrels of eons ago could be revisited for dirt in the dung-heap, or any troublesome coworker could stand accused, however innocent or cosmopolitan. A bird flying at night and chirping is misconstrued as heading for a convention of witches. No evidence to prove anything but a giddy, cultural festival of inquisition pervades.

At another level, however Christian or Islamic, some family members, in desperation can consult prophets, traditional medicants, shamans, native or witch doctors, and fortune tellers, ad infinitum. Valuable, scanty family resources are expended on procuring goats, rams or cows, herbs accompanied with sacrificial chants to placate ancestors, spiritual pantheons and also to ward off perceived or imagined enemies. All these may not have anything to do with the biology of the disease in question, though one must grant that some genuine traditional medications or fortifications do work in some instances.

During the tense moments of my pestilence, some literary colleagues got wind of my situation. You cannot seal it up in a jar forever, however hermetically. It will bubble to the surface. Many called when I was in the hospital. Others called the family at home, sometimes repeatedly. Such honorable mentions are due Tanure Ojaide (poet, critic), Charles Mann (Linguist and Critic), Isidore Okpewho (critic and novelist), Niyi Osundare (poet, critic), Rashesed Na' Allah (writer and critic), Bayo and Nike Lawal (statistician; linguist),

Odun Balogun (writer and critic), Ode Ogede (writer and critic), Sunday Babaoye (doctor), Dr Balogun Chike Obi (phycist), Femi Ojo-ade (French specialist and critic), and Dr. (Mrs.) Ugonna Chike Obi (neonatologist).

Stage II

While I was recovering from my first affliction, a silent but potent expeditionary force assailed and ambushed me. I woke up one morning in the summer of 99 and went to the bathroom to clean up for school. The room twirled and appeared upside down. I staggered and could not maintain my balance. My head spun and was shaking. I must be having vertigo. So I thought. What the hell is this O God! Is this the beginning of the end! So I exasperated. I could not raise my right hand to brush my teeth. It was stiff. I could not comb my hair nor tie the strings of my shoes. I managed after several attempts to dress up and drove to school. Driving became a tug of war. While I meant to stay within the lane, my head would order the car to move to the right in a possible calamitous collision with cars plying on the right. I sweated profusely to make it to school. I did not last the next three hours. A friend drove me to meet my doctor, some thirty miles away from school. Alas it was my doctor's day off- Dr Robert Felder, a very nice special man in my life, at Kaiser Hospital in Carlsbad, California. A young-female-tendril primary doctor examined me. "I think you have a TIA, Professor Tayo." "What's that?" I inquired ignorantly. "That is a stroke without a stroke. You are very lucky. It came and went away. Your face did not collapse. Your right side is mildly affected. Your speech is very clear and strong, but I cannot allow you to go home. You must see a specialist right away for treatment." I was transferred to Palomar Hospital in Escondido, a few kilometers away. My family heard from the hospital at 10 pm, I was hospitalized. Here I remained for the next four days. Dr. Felder and associates paraded to my room almost daily. I received blood thinners, did MRI's at the Imaging Institute, and got better and finally walked again. I received instructions in physical therapy, diet and exercise. I went home. The hospital arranged my transportation.

Days later, Dr. Jay Rosenberg, the neurology consultant at Kaiser Zion, near my home in Old Town, San Diego called. I went to see him. The man is a breathing encyclopedia of medical linguistics. He examined me and talked in rapid monologues as he recorded himself on the computer. I was animated with him. He won my heart. He was vertical and adept with language and knowledge of medicine. He was dynamic and sharp. I became his disciple without hesitation.

"Tayo, what is going on here? You are still a young man, and you have been through so much already this year. I am glad to see you, still smiling. That's character." He made his recommendation that Dr David Levy, the neurosurgeon should see me for the next stage. Dr. Levy then recommended a brain surgery procedure if cerebral angiogram confirmed their suspicion. The offending artery must be dilated to permit blood to flow. "The procedure is called stenting, and is very risky. If we are lucky, it can be conveniently done. We will put a balloon into the narrowing one of the important arteries that go to the brain, to open it up, just as we do to the heart. You will be under observation for the next 48 hours in the hospital after surgery."

Appointments were made. I went for the arteriogram on the 12th of October 1999. Some poems will attest to that encounter in this collection. I stayed in the hospital for almost eight hours. My cousin, Martin Akinfosile, followed me to and from the hospital. Soon after arriving there, I was asked to disrobe to my birthday suit and wear a nameless hospital garment. A bed awaited me. There I lay and received an intravenous line. Soon I made it to the theater of "Special procedures" or something to that effect. The gadgetry in there shook my confidence a little, seeing very large cauldron sized cameras and monitors and a miscellaneous assortment of instruments. I was transferred to a special bed with a tiny forked headrest. They held down my head with tape. My entire body was covered with very heavy cellophane drapes. They covered my nose with an oxygen belching tube. It was a smoke screen for something else. I must have been asleep for the following hours without knowing it. I forgot everything. They had incised the femoral artery in the groin in my sleep without pain. My groin area had been shaved. I located the spot of incision through which they fed their dye, the next morning. When I woke up from the surgery, they took X-ray pictures galore. They rattled commands to make sure, perhaps that I was still breathing. The X-ray demanded it.

I felt groggy. My head was woozy. I had planned to teach at the National University that evening. The doctor vetoed me. My legs could hardly carry me. The evening closed in and Martin was permitted to ship me home. I slumped onto our living room couch. There I slept till 2:45 am when my daughter tiptoed in to wake me up.

"Daddy, why aren't you in your bed? I am cold, cover me up in my room." I trudged and thrashed around to fetch her an additional blanket. I enjoy doing those family chores for my child.

My wife believes in God and the hospital, especially Dr Felder, our friend, that's the extent of her concerns. Femi, my daughter mused aloud, "Daddy, please don't die. God will take care of you. If something happened to you, I would have nobody to trust and feel free to tell my secrets", usually primary school rascalities.

My Dean, Renee Kilmer at Southwestern, was always kind to me. I had no trouble getting permission for my hospital visits or getting sponsored for my conferences. Bertha, our gorgeous black secretary with her Hispanic counterparts, Mariana called me "Africa" endearingly, and they closely monitored my delicacy with soothing inquiries. Jane Tassi, a sectional head of our

Department Computer Services is an angel. You have the impression that she is a feminist and an intellectual in her own right. She is enormously warm and gentle with me. Always concerned and worried. She brought me her late father's walking stick to steady my gait. I will never forget any of them. They touched me with their enormous humanity. Some Americans are so very special.

Stage III

In the evening of Friday the 15th of October 1999, Dr David Levy called and said: "Tayo, I have examined the film of your cerebral angiogram. You have a stenosis in the brain- a narrowing of the artery. Surgery is the only way to go, if we are to arrest the problem on time. I have consulted with many experts and we all agreed that surgery is the best choice. The prospect looks very good for your kind of condition. We have done 15 to date. The procedure as you know, is called angioplasty stenting. The surgery will take place in New York. You and I will fly to New York where they are preparing for us, if you agree with our assessment. There are other experts waiting for us there. The hospital will take care of everything. You will stay behind for a day or two for observation before you fly back to San Diego. I will fly back here immediately after the surgery. We are planning to leave here on Sunday, the 5th of December. Early Monday morning of the following day, the operation will take place. Please get back in touch with me as soon as possible, having done all the consultations, you may need."

"Thank you, doctor. I am very excited at this prospect, risky as it is. As we say back home, the goat will finally kill the leopard."
"We'll keep our fingers crossed. All things being equal, we are good and confident. Bye for now."
Dr Ugonna Chike Obi, a very good friend of my wife, and also the wife of a colleague advised her to ask me to call Dr. Bola Oyeshiku, a Nigerian neurosurgeon, in Atlanta for an additional opinion. The doctor called Dr. Levy. They both agreed that the surgery was most vital and urgent

A new twist develops as my world turns:

"Gring! Gring!" the phone rang.
"Hello"
"Dr. Levy here"
"What's up Doc?"
I was a bit apprehensive because the surgery in New York had been postponed once. We had the 27th of December yet to be confirmed, but some days later the 13th was chosen to be suitable. On this present call, the news

was ominous, only for a minute. Dr. Levy did not allow its impact to register.

"Tayo, Buffalo turned us down. They would not give us their cooperation as planned."

"But why doctor?"

"They are afraid that the surgery is too complicated. The artery blocked in the brain is too curvy to be reached. You know what? There is also good news. I only wanted their collaboration since this procedure is relatively new. But as heavens would have it, I am ahead of them in the experience of treating this problem. I am confident that despite all the risks, we can safely get you through here in San Diego. The technology I'll use for you is far superior to theirs, which they were going to use for you. I'll go ahead and order my colleagues for their views. We will meet again soon after arrangements are made. We'll then schedule the surgery. We have the option of a bypass, but that may not be necessary. All operations are risky. I am confident, however, of our expertise, so don't worry. We don't need New York at all. When does school start for your? After Christmas?"

"January 10th."

"That is good. Plenty of time to recover."

"Thank you doctor, I leave it all to you. You have been kind and concerned with me, and I cannot ask for more. I am lucky to be receiving this attention. After all, you have no intention to kill me or maim my health. I am eternally grateful."

"We are here for you. See you soon."

I shed a few private tears as the doctor dropped the phone. I was hurt that New York thought me a basket case. If that were so, they would've abandoned me to the throes of precipitate and imminent death, if I were their resident patient in Buffalo. As my doctor said, "There is a great blessing sometimes behind every disappointment. I can now do that which I do best."

As I calmed down, I hardly knew when I composed the work below. I typed it and took it to the notary to notarize and distribute copies, except my wife's copy, which I'll hold until the moment of my departure. I enveloped it and placed it on her table with a note of thanks for all the years- just in case I never have any opportunity to say, "I love and appreciate you."

Brain surgery

To my wife, children, and family at-large....

If anything were to happen to me during this procedure, or there after, please do not sue or exploit the kindness of Dr. David Levy and his team or the Kaiser establishment. While Buffalo turned us down amidst this turbulence in the sea of life, Dr. Levy, despite the risks, is courageous to put his expertise on the line to help me. He meant well and this I appreciate beyond reprieve. He should not suffer reprisals or disrepute for his altruism. Besides, he will do his utmost to achieve a fair result. May the heavens and my ancestors help him. David, do all you can to help my family, just in case…Especially my daughter who is only ten. Dr. Nitahara, Urology, Kaiser, Otay Mesa and I, had once discussed her education at the University of California San Diego, my alma mater. He will organize something for her future, if it needs be. Thanks to you all.

Tayo
November 28, 1999

A personal note to my wife:

I want to thank you from the bottom of my heart for all the years. While you were asleep or busy quarreling and giving me the silent treatment, sometimes my tears were busy silently standing on my pillow. This might be our last togetherness. I thank you for your devotion and courage. I never can tell what tomorrow will bring in this situation. Take care of our child, Femi. I love you all. It had been a very jolly ride. My immense and immeasurable gratitude.

Eternally,
Tayo

The saga continues in this diary of events

By 1 pm this Wednesday, the 30th of November, Dr. David Levy gave me a call. The twist continued. He had met his departmental executive assembly of medic-nerds on my case specifically.

"They counseled further tests. "he announced. "And we agreed to take it easy because this is a very risky undertaking. Dr. Jay Rosenberg was there. The doctors said that we should refer you to see our cardiologist, to ensure the healthy functioning of your heart before we proceed. Might there be a problem to be discovered anew. We even considered alternative medication to surgery if it would help alleviate your condition. We want to do the best for you. If your heart poses no problem, we may end up doing the operation. But let's attend to unexpected problems now. For further necessary investigation, I'll want you to see me and also Dr. Rosenburg. You will hear from the cardiologist's nurse within a week. If they are late calling, give me a call so that we urge them to expedite. I'll ask my nurse to make arrangements for you to see me. You are fine for now. It takes a long time for the artery to narrow further. Let's take care of possible obstacles first, O.K.? See you soon."

After a few minutes of sweaty rush through my pores, I realized that I am really very luck. All these experts are treading slowly to not make any mistakes on me. I was neither depressed nor anguished. Any fatal blow may be irretrievable. Caution is the anthem, they know but I don't know what they do know. I booked an appointment with Rosenberg for the following days. Come to think of it, maybe Buffalo was right after all.

Time will tell.

Dunni, one of my siblings, never wanted this surgery. She was weepingly vociferous against it.

"Oh no brother!" she anguished. She committed the matter to prayer, as did many other relatives.

"I'm not in a hurry to die, far from it. I feel the spiritual universe is watching over me. For the moment however, I am between a rock and a hard place. There is no escape from this reality. I am truly in the eye of the storm. Only a survivor knows the burden.

October 19, 1999
To Whom It May Concern:

Tayo Olafioye has been under my medical care since early this calendar year. In March he underwent extensive surgery for the treatment of prostate. Since his surgery, he has endured the routine postoperative changes, which have necessitated that he not work for 6 weeks from the time of surgery. In addition, he has needed prolonged use of multiple medications. Mister Olafioye will need continued monitoring at regular intervals to assess his progress from the time of surgery.

Kenneth Nitahara, MD
Kaiser Permanente, San Diego

I kept my appointment with Dr. Rosenburg. He did not mince a word. His objection was uncompromising. He viewed surgery dimly. "The brain is the engine room of the body. To tinker with it, is to invite what you were trying to prevent. The blocked artery is right inside your brain, the ravine of it. If you were my son, I would be hesitant. Caution first, clarity second. Even if your heart were sound, I'll still object. Dr. Levy and I have agreed in conference to treat you by other means. Not this risky operation." His submission virtually killed the enthusiasm. And now, everybody believes their unspoken anxieties.

In time, this cyclone will pass and it will be history. I look forward to an effective treatment, so that life can be full and jolly again. One never truly knows how golden life is until one squeezes through the eye of a needle without the pestilence or ravages of infirmities in the chambers. Those who achieve sudden expiration owe a trillion gratitudes to death. They never see their lives ebb before them. They never have to struggle to breathe. They never suffer the agonies of excruciating discomfort. They never see their loved ones and friends whittle in agony, helplessly within, for their sake. Nobody dies alone.

*Note: Today, Friday, the 10th of December 1999, my brain surgery was officially postponed for four months, at least to give all contesting approaches and proprieties time to breathe. The doctors held their departmental conference on me (consultation really in other cultures' medical tradition). They arranged their cardiologist to examine my heart. They scheduled older patients with similar conditions or prognosis, to blaze the procedure first before my turn. Thus the various surgical teams could assess their successes, failures or handicaps. Each consultant signaled active caution.. I am very thrilled for it beyond imaginable measures. What the heck! You only live once. I am enjoying all the fuss over me. The doctors met with me after their conference, I was told that for the time being, I must stay on my various medications. The matter must be resolved. It cannot dangle forever like a plant without roots. I cannot manage any more disaster. There is a limit to human endurance.

My book as a stroke of hope is a metaphor. Double, triple or quadruple entendre. It hits at many levels of meanings and interpretations. It was a stroke of discovery that my affliction was caught at its very early stage, gathering seismic tremor to explode. It was a stroke of celestial determination that I ran into Kaiser's expert physicians who care. They refused to count me a statistic of waste, which was a stroke of providential and ancestral interposition. My stroke was mild, thereby providing me the chance to fully recover. Many are not so lucky. I do not dangle in spacey unreality without roots or diminished capacity as a human being, a carcass of my former vibrancy. I could have been six feet under. It was a stroke of fate, and an accident of hope, that I have a second chance. To die a hero or a martyr is meaningless. Life is my hope. Hope is my future. I must take care of it because I must be there. This smacks a stroke of survival and retrieval not helpless hopelessness or hopeless helplessness.

The concept of a stroke that incapacitates or destroys, being a subject of speculative hope, is in itself an irony, possibly an oxymoron as well. This is my paradox; my eloquent dilemma.

Current Medical Advance in the USA
David Levy, MD
Department of Neurosurgery, Kaiser Permanete.
San Diego, California

Re: Tayo Olafioye

Tayo Olafioye is a fifty-five year old right-handed Nigerian English professor who developed episodes of balance difficulties, weakness and numbness of his right arm and leg in June, 1999. This resulted in some difficulty walking. Within two weeks, his motor function and ability to walk had returned but not to its full capacity. His right arm function has not yet fully returned. He developed fatigue easily but has further episodes of weakness or numbness since June 1999. He was placed on blood thinners since that time. On examination, he appears to have good strength in both lower extremities and he walks without difficulty.

When I first met Tayo Olafioye, he was obviously a kind and gentle man. At his relatively young age for these medical problems, he was coping well with difficulty. His studies included an MRI angiography, which demonstrated a high grade narrowing of his left middle artery which corresponds to the area of the stroke. It was obvious that he had some residual weakness of his right arm, thus signaling some neural depth in the region of the left middle cerebral artery. The angiogram demonstrated the narrowing was significant.

There has been a movement recently to treat patients with high grade stenosis of their intracranial arteries with angioplasty and, most recently, intracranial stenting. An intracranial stent is a slotted tube that can be expanded using a balloon which expands the artery and narrowing, while the stent, once expanded, does not allow the artery to contract again, keeping the stenosis open and allowing greater blood flow through the stenosis. There is currently no intracranial stent that is FDA approved. However, there is one stent specifically designed for intracranial vessels that is currently in trials in Buffalo, New York, under the direction of Dr. L.N. Hopkins.

I presented Dr. Olafioye with the options that included treating this with blood thinning medication, which he would need to stay on for the remainder of his life, or an attempt at intracranial stent placement. The procedure is a new procedure and, thus, the risks are not fully known. The experience we have with angioplasty and stenting in the arteries of the heart as well in other arteries in the body generally yields good results, however, given the fact that the arteries of the brain are so small and so thin walled, a separate trail is necessary. Therefore, with Dr. Olafioye's approval and with his full understanding of the risks involved in undertaking such treatment, we'll plan to fly to Buffalo, New York to attempt to place a stent in the middle left middle cerebral artery. At this time, it is not known, with his torturous anatomy, we will be able to even bring the device to the area of narrowing. However, an attempt will be made.

A poet facing life, death, and prosperity

Often, perhaps too often, we forget that certain people—professionals, professors, poets—are mere mortals, like the rest of us, doomed to fall victim to that implacable grand master connected of destruction, Death. However, what distinguishes a handful of individuals from the vast majority is, the quality of life, the determination to defy death, to stand up and shout a resounding No! No, to cowardice. No to connivance. No, to corruption. For, this acts an attitude of revolt, nay, of revolution, or not positive in isolation; they are symbolic of an overall philosophy encompassing everything that comes together in the complex whole called Life. Life, not everlasting, but short, of a season. Life, potentially innocent, sweet, marked by moral rectitude, and a consciousness of, as well as a commitment to, values that lift humanity to the zenith of achievement and accomplishment. Yet, Life, dragged down to the depth of disease and destruction by locusts and vampires and vultures disguised as humans. And, the real human being are compelled to choose between the condition of slaves, victims of those doctors of death, and the status of courageous revolutionaries, fighting for freedom, and prepared to pay the ultimate price so that they, by all means necessary, may become immortals and annals of prosperity. A contradiction in terms, one can hear some cynics sneer through the yellow—a sure sign of cowardice!

Those that are fortunate to read *A Stroke-of Hope* will have a ready answer for such naysayers. Here is a poet, a meer mortal, doing something strange: He reveals to his audience his innermost thoughts, at that instant when most would prefer to keep their secrets secret; when they would rather guard their privacy jealousy and obsessively, in order not to reveal their deficiencies, in order not to tumble down from their heights of hypocrisy and ego-tripping. And, this poet goes further, by making of his audience, at first, reluctant companions in his journey through existential hell; and then, with his poetic skills of making magic with words and striking the chord of communality well learnt form his African culture, winning over his audience to share in his escape from that hell to the point where , together, they can look death in the eye, with defiance, but not absolutely, not with the demonic demeanor of dictators so common to his ancestral continent. In a word, Tayo Olafioye's poems reveal his thoughts, his fears and despair, in the midst of his season of "stroke without a stroke: his doubts, as to whether he would survive the onslaught, or succumb; his rising courage, and (almost) convictions, that is, the hope, that he will not die, because he has too much to live for. Family, Friends, Students, and Society, the society that is the human universe but, precisely, that society that begins and ends in his Africa; for Tayo knows full well that he is "always an African at heart." (MY EPITAPH WHENEVER)

A particularly striking aspect of the collection is the preamble to the poetry, where the poet presents the biography of his illness, and the reviews of the three doctors-surgeons engaged in his care. As already affirmed, one's first reaction might be, that this is strange, too strange to behold. Nonetheless, without this introduction, one cannot fully comprehend the poems. The introductory details set the stage, as it were or, indeed, provided the surface existential panorama, for the drama that unfolds in the poems. Those descriptions of the patient's condition—fears, hopes, hopelessness, faith and, especially, love at the edge of the abyss—allows us to empathize with the patient-poet, to share in his story and conclude, as he does, that "whoever has not died does not know the joy of living."

The body of poems is divided into four parts, each identified with a hospital room, and a major theme. The first is "Room 211-On Illness." The poems here are the most intimate and excruciating of all, being the most central to the patient's condition, and the most personal to him and his psyche. His reactions to the surgeons' opinions and actions. His contemplation of pain in all its ramifications, and the professionalism of his doctors. Most importantly, the journey from Life, to the gates of Death, and back. "I am not in a hurry to die, far from it. I feel the spiritual universe is watching over me," the poet confirms to a sibling totally scared and opposed to surgery. That determination to live is aided and, indeed, encouraged and pushed to the fore by the surgeons, "super gods" and "wizard":

Without them
Where shall we be?

As he does in quite a number of poems in the collection, Tayo uses the format of dichotomy and contrast to examine and explore the constant struggle to survive. While surgeons symbolize survival, the earthen soil represents the force of control and destruction:

Never sick
But devours daily, in sumptuous gulps.
(SURGEONS)

Metaphor is also a constant. Cancer is " stealth bomber of the physique," to whom the poet pays homage, reluctantly and ironically. "To know [prostate cancer] is to smell death." In the poem, "The mechanics of Physique," Tayo describes himself as

The guest of ill heath
In the home of repairs.

The "home" could be one of healing, but also one of the horror of death. Hence, while praising the surgeons, the poet does not eschew the presence of the murderous Enemy, Death. "let me trot again" finds him at the crossroads between Life and Death, ready to go under the knife, the same instrument used in carving up a chicken and in cutting out cancer from the human body. Thus, one is struck by the inextricable link between life and death.

The, Hope begins to loom, large.

I hope to listen
To the sounds of paradise
If I make it there.

Would that mean that the patient is prepared to quit this vale of tears, and soar to life everlasting in the great beyond? One finds references to religion spread through the pages of this collection. Happily that those are passing moments, surpassed by others that declare hope in life, this life, here and now. Such hope is expressed in the poem, "at that moment of departure" dedicated to the poet's daughter, and in the poems written for his three surgeons. The "Poetry of Death" admits the finality of the life, but without resigning himself to that fate.

In the surgeon poems, there are metaphors galore, expressing and emphasizing the strengths of those individuals fighting death to the finish.

You are the tiger who strides stealthily
Not of cowardice
But of knowledge of the landscape.

Such usage of animals—a reference point for Tayo's Africanity—abounds in the text. Tiger, elephants, lions, as well as myth and legends, and deities, come up as a reminder of the wisdom of a culture much maligned by the western masters "Prayer" is proof of the viability of African culture, and religion. Just as "genius knows no color or race," so does religion refuse to categorize any cult as superior to others.

That remark brings us to Part Two of the book, "Room 34-Nigerian Condition." The question would be, how come a patient combating death, would be thinking of some faraway place called Nigeria, when he should be using all his energy—physical and psychological—to fight his own battle? The response is a no-brainer for the committed artist: Victory in the personal battle can only be meaningful in the knowledge that the sickness of the Nigerian (his home) society is extracted, like cancer! For, the reality of Nigeria is enough to fall sick. The country, reputedly "giant of Africa," has been reduced to the stature of a gnome by dictator Abacha, "a veritable evil." The Khailif of ritual death," and his horde of "moral lepers," "cancer-invalids," mired in criminality, corruption, greed, and graft, and "the arrogance of invincibility." This feeling of immortality subtly links the second section to the first; only of course, while the poet recognizes his human frailty as he struggles to survive the onslaught of Death, these nitwits misruling a country turned into their serfdom, know no reason to stench their megalomania. But, unlike the poet, a survivor, Abacha, an anti-Christ figure "never made to walk on water," is suddenly cut down by Death: "God's true coup silenced the beast." Furthermore, the hope fitfully explored in the first part of the collection, now comes into full bloom. "Hope breathes new life," the poet exalts.

Today is resurrection and retrieval
The people bellow their hallelujahs.

Nonetheless, just as the patient cannot forget that his struggle is a continuous process, so also are the people of Nigeria cautioned "do not forget." Even with the coronation of a new civilian (once military) president who vows to eradicate corruption in the land, the poet maintains a wait-and-see attitude. "They Start Again" recounts the parliamentarians' decadent behavior (can a tiger change its spots?). The poet-turned-doctor prescribes for sick Nigeria: "service without pay."

The country, terribly sick and comatose
In the hospital of anomie
Needs all medications of cure.

From the Nigerian patient, we move to Part Three, "Room 406-Interntional Scene." Here, evil also prevails, although the profundity does not approach that exemplified by Nigeria. "Faces of infamy," with a refrain reminiscent of African orature's call and response, lists various scenes of human sickness, "where[reign] hopelessness, and helplessness, forgetfulness and death." Death is a Presence, with the disappearance of some famous ones ("The Sun Also Sets in Caleot," about the death of John Kennedy, Jr.) reminding us that the Enemy knows no class. Which does not diminish the madness of ego-trippers carrying stone in place of heart ("The Cubism of Mayhem"). But all is not lost, as we read "Mandela." ...Yet, one wonders whether bidding good-bye to the noble man, "the tallest tree in Africa," the most courageous of this millennium, " and witnessing the end of "this millennium of pains," would at once mean the end of all our sufferings in Africa.

The final section "Room 512-Cultural Garden," proffers one possibility for rehabilitating Africa's humanity, through Culture. "Iwo Festivals," with poetic dexterity and a humor rare in the collection, recounts the triumph of Yoruba culture over Christianity. The pastor of Ilutitun (Yoruba: new city), symbol of modernity, "a western civilized idiot," leads unwary women to their doom when they are urged to disobey age-old laws of traditional religion. In this section, Tayo makes quite a number of thought provoking statement, mostly anchored on the wisdom oh his culture. "Any society without myth or festival is dead." (Iwo Festival)

Nobody needs reality
More than those
Who have none to give.
(OH! NO! MY SON BECOMES A GIRL!)
It makes no difference
If a man sees a snake
And a woman kills it. (Ibid.)

Pronouncements of human values based upon quality of character, viability of culture, and non-sexism, they express a position already found in Tayo's published writings. The question of women's condition would, no doubt, interest many a western reader. Caution: No Eurocentric feminism in this poetry; rather, there is an African humanism underscoring each gender's qualities and roles, and the ultimate complementarity within the totality of existential and experiential firmament. Thus, the poet, as a father, is not ashamed to fawn upon his beautiful little girl; nor is he hesitant to draw a portrait of his wife and her knack for disguise and mystery. The image of complementarity is marvelously captured in "Kama Kevin King," in which a black couple (king and queen) raises their "son of the gods," a continuity of their shared nobility.

The poem, "Islands of Spirits in African Cosmos," depicts our pantheons and deities,

Creative or destructive
Blessing or a curse
Demons or gods.

In paying homage to these spirits, the poet returns to the beginning of his journey, to once again raise the essential questions about Life and Death. The difference now is, that he has conquered fear, and hopelessness.

The original title of the book was *My Season of Inconvenience*. Upon reading the text, one is convinced of the superiority of the new title. The poetry itself constitutes a stroke, as "of the pen" or of the artist's brush, putting down on paper feelings and ideas that bear an important message for the community. Stroke, too, as regards a sudden occurrence, as "of luck," reminding us that the poet is fortunate to be here with us, as we are to be in a position to read these soul-searching verses. And, of course, stroke, as that never expected stoppage, and seizure, of bodily functions, immobilizing all motors, transforming an active man into a static and stagnant liability. When combined with hope, the picture becomes complex, but comprehensive, and complete, as human life, before the dreaded Death.

A word about the genesis of this essay. When Tayo contacted me to do it, I sensed in his voice a certain urgency, a certain desperation. I hesitated to accept. Maybe out of formless fear, maybe due to the desire to keep a safe distance from things treating Death. Maybe out of certain cowardice. But, then. I thought more about it all. We met only a couple of years ago, but have known each other for much longer, through our works, as critics and creative artists born and bred in the same sick society; as victims of oppressors in a system suffocating and stifling life, and desirous of destroying its own children; and as survivors refusing to quit the struggle.

So, I ended up accepting to write the essay. Now that I have read the text, and written above, from the heart, I feel blessed, and gratified. My sensitivity has been refueled (and let us hope the pumps in our dear Nigeria never again go dry!) and, I daresay, my life has been given more meaning, even as I know categorically that we all must die one day. That is our destiny. Fortunately for Tayo, the poet, the work, concrete, constructed in a language all his own, with heart and soul, will live for prosperity.

Thank you, Tayo. Ire o.

Femi Ojo-Ade

Surgeons

Smart
some think: as super gods
maybe, super nerds
they are everything—
without them
where shall we be?
Only wizards talk diseases
or strain blood.

This earthen-soil is never sick
but devours daily, sumptuous gulps:
earthquakes today,
hurricanes tomorrow,
volcano's viscosity,
floods or tornadoes seasonally.
Its incubus promotes human terminations—
all, mincemeats in its rich esophagus.

It takes wizards to stem its pulls.
they can use a hatchet
to ease a fly
from a maladied head.

Tribute to the Stealth Bomber

Prostate—
the enemy of Eros
the god of Libido
the son of Aphrodite
exponential potentate
supreme power of evil
the prince of darkness,
phallic god unrefined,
man's most dreaded scourge
whose malevolent arrow-cancer
shivers the spine
most mortal males—
mere mention alone:
brands hot iron of fear
ON the mind
I salute you!

To know you
is to smell death.
or asphyxiate the passages of life.
silent attacks your mode.
dry semen, your elixir.
Supreme power of evil
malevolent prince of darkness
I salute you!
You renege attacks
where fed-a-right
but they court
your wrath and pestilence—
those ignoramuses who offer
tobacco, snuff, red meat, hot drinks
carcinogenous beverages and such pollutants
articles of unfilial hospitality
to your Most Dreaded Eminence—
through gully channels of the esophagus
you hibernate in ambush
fast-spreading your tentacles
in the streams of their veins—
never to forgive
but to launch reprisals
you, the stealth bomber of the physique

I salute you—
crown prince of decimation
yes, almighty doctors—
try to outwit your smartness:
they send their Chemo and radios
to repel your advance.
there you are—
smiling in waiting,
knowing, conquest is yours,
however long, the sanitary campaigns,
you will ravage everything—
the phallus and the hospitals
mere shells of lives before.
But surely,
physicians are the warriors of courage
they will assassinate your malevolence.

At That Moment of Departure

My nine-year-old was at school
I left her a note; my heart fell;
Good-bye my darling
As I go under the knife.
I pray to see you again
For which: I shall be grateful.
If not:
My time must have been done
I left you and mommy, phone numbers to call.
Remember always,
Daddy loves you to the end
And will never forget you.

You are the pupil
Of my eyes.
Our bond: no dictionary can define
Our blood: only Nature can refine
The language it speaks
Or the oneness it portends.

Fofo—my only one of history
Foyin-Femi—one who puts honey into my life
Good-bye for now,
I hope to see you again, soon
If Fate so designs.
The hunter who has only one arrow
Does not shoot aimlessly.

Let Me Trot Again

I am on the road
Through the jagged paths of the unconscious,
Where forced to sleep
The stony lapse into no re-turn.
The knife, they say—
Not savory or jolly on the neck of a chicken,
If only I had a choice
None of my own
As no line remains
In a sandstorm.

I hope to listen
To the sounds of paradise
If I make it there.
This jagged road to the unconscious,
The stony sleep into surgery.
Will I see the Christian light
At the end of the tunnel?
Or, simply the fellowship of sufferers?

This must be the research
Into the religion of death.
Maybe will be too leaden to care
If life exists on the other side—
Or simply, two worlds of disconnect?
These six hours of butchered sleep
In the landscaping of my abdomen.
The silent holocaust of my parts

I have taken a train
To the gate
Between life and death
To mind, a messy chore.

The moon that wanes today
Will be full tomorrow.
So God shooed me away—
Sinners like me.
His port was full, unprocessed.
"Not yet," my ancestors snapped.
Calmly, I turned to the resurrection

Of sleep-wake
Confused and dazed:
"Where am I?" I sneered.
Arrogant again, you see! Forgetting that—
Life gives its own brand of justice

Till then let me trot here for a little longer.

The Poetry of Death

Images of the mind:
Weird, nightly dreams—
Revolutions of the maimed,
Games that sickness plays
In the bed of discomfort.
Maybe not the bull,
But has got every horn
The bull employs.

Incisions and myriad tubes,
Bindings a-taut every stretch
All over the place.
Sometimes you wish as a candidate
Despair can be temporary
But the river must flow its course.
One must know
When one has pepper
In one's eyes

Tossing and turning
Groaning and moaning.
Dazed all night long
In formless imaginings
These are:
Many steps beyond the pale,
Bottles galore to drain
The catheters of inconvenience.

Only that some nurses are angels
Touch and voices are salvation,
To whiff the pains away.
He who is courteous
Is not a fool.
Illness, the great reminder of man's
Air-weight fragility.
When the time comes,
No man or fate can revise
The irrationality of death.

We try so vainly
To make our shadows dance

And the elephant to somersault
In the fiendish poetry of Death.
Or jig Ijala*:
The hunters' monodies of finality.

*Ijala-Hunters' traditional oral poetry

The mechanics of physique

I am the guest of ill-health
In the home of repairs.
Moaning in silence
As the mechanics of physique
Salivate to vet their art on me.
We are many
Looking for tap roots
On the tree-tops of hope,
Each summarizing what life has meant.
Nothing matters now,
All the faces speak
The language of despair,
The outside is all-dark,
Prison without sun in our hearts,
This is the last stop
On our train ride
To success or failure,
Life and death,
Survival or hopelessness
Renaissance or life-of -no-return.
When the roots of a tree
Begin to decay
They spread death
To the branches
My mind was a messy grave
As I whispered good-bye to my family.
Here we were—passengers
Waiting to board the planes of ill health,
This surgical admitting room.
Our passports and papers stamped
Clipped, handed each for the guillotine.
To think that this might be the last.
How this unknown paralyzed me
Such a moment of life's disconnect
A journey of no return.
An eerie feeling
I lay on the gurney at their command
Without clothes of fashion to impress
Just my birthday suit
For the mechanics to re-tool.

A fat lady trudged in
Kindly she was and professional
Introduced a liquid kiss to my vein,
That was the last I remembered.
Thus began in earnest
The prostate journey to death or renewal.
No C-word* or visitor in my mold
Told me in the wake after
Twenty-four hours of stony sleep.
"Where are we?" I asked
"When shall we do it?"
"Done since yesterday," the answer came
some eyes stared over me
"We removed the large tomato
that pressed your channels.
Your sex nerves preserved.
Lucky you," the doctor enthused.

Soon I noticed, my chest oppressed
My tummy very leaden.
My head swam in cartoons of impossibilities
Nothing jelled in spacey unreality.
Three bottles and tubes labyrinth my nerves.
Drain as lifesavers.

Hats off to the nurses
Truly the angels of mercy.
Love patients and predicaments;
Master the dirty jobs,
No one else will be decent to do.
I shall be home my chant
I shall be home my hope
Where I shall hug my special ones,
At the barnyard of survival,
The shrine of ancestral gratitude,
To live once again.
Home is the sweet return
From the wilds of ill-heath.

*C-word = cancer

Dr. Kenneth Nitahara
Kaiser, San Diego, California

Oracle, Mediciner, Diviner—
Size is no threat
To the labyrinth depths
Of your mind.
In the theatre of body mechanics
No Einstein can match your worth.
You are the tiger who strides stealthily,
Not of cowardice
But of knowledge of the landscape.
My surgeon-urologist, extra-ordinaire
A friend who tells your face
When your insides are ugly.

Moves smartly
To dike the corrosions of death.
Wherever possible, you safely
Rework the landscape
To save my breath.

My hat is off to your genius.
May your name stand erect
In the annals of distinction.
Genius knows no color or race.

It knows you.

I Will Be History

Ever since my surgery
I fear death,
The inevitability of it all,
Like night and day.
Only a flicker between here and the beyond.
The pity of it all,
No escape from reality.
Right now, I wish I am eighteen again.
Any overnight stay at the hospital
These days, gives the jitters—
It might be the last.
Should not be sorry
But, I am, for life is not only short
But also fictive
To have no enemies or excess
Is equivalent to wealth
And longevity
I envision laying prostate
My eternal sleep.
My children sobbing my no return
I weep the pain in their hearts
Their loneliness in sorrow
Helpless, hapless, hopeless.
But time creates acceptance
Soon I become their memory.
Perhaps fatherly lectures
Or examples become their catechisms.
Will be dazed for a while
But, it will pass
They already know:
However heavy the pail of life
Can lift it anyway
With diligence and luck.
A season would come
When I will ride the streets
For the last time,
Or trail the environs
Or dine a restaurant.
Then, I will be history
After a season.
You have to appreciate.

Pain: The Vilest Weed That Grows

This weed, vilest in the mind
If wetted by the rain of bitterness.
Yet, nobody remembers pain
But I doff my hat
For its occupation.
If physical, its throb can be choking
If psychological, a state of mind,
It can be numbing
Or unremittingly jolting
To deaden the nerves.
Some can be so biting,
They ride the hurricanes of revenge.
Without retaliation, evil
Would one day be
Extinct from the earth.

Prayer

The magic of human will
the pillar of abstract faith
thrasher of psychological fix
author of the healing mantras
ally of the shattered peace
unseen messenger of hope
omnipotent eternal essence
mender of the wounded trust
tailor of shredded plans
deliverer from the seaweeds of life
lifter of burdened dreams
filler of empty homes
shaman of human miseries
manna for nameless orphans
miracle of uncharted seas
doctor of the broken hearts
the dove of the hunted life
finisher of human endeavors
conjurer of alien hounds

Vilest Weed, Part II

A medical oxymoron that resurrects
Those in the esophagus of death,
Or those who breathe pain terminally
In the throes of the hospice—
The halfway house to eternity.

This euphemistic weed,
And angel of mercy
Commands respectable clients:
Cancer: Glaucoma, AIDS, nausea ad infinitum.
Who says evil has no good?
San Francisco leads the Vanguard of
Enlightenment
In spite of remonstrations
From aficionados and most medical gurus.

Every revolution is born to a revolt.

Wagging the Dog

In this season of inconvenience
Harsh words thrash my veins
Some tongues wag my veins
They say I am a damaged dog
Even my wife echoed my friends.
She should know better
For a while after prostate
Every nerve went on vacation
The blood refused to pump.
With blood clotting the brain
I was lucky to manage
A stroke without a stroke.
All my vitals were normal
But my stamina ebbed; my gait slowed.
In that kind of inclemency
Who wants to flip
From the mountaintop?
"You have been through much this year Tayo,"
the doctor said "Take it easy"
it's foolhardy to tumble
From humping, contrary
To the meaning of viagra—but
It worked! And it did.
First, neurologist arranged physical therapies
They were a god-send
Courage is the father of success.
I snapped from being a jelly fish flax
To being a belly of bouncing rubber,
Better to be a damaged dog and breathing, than
Being a strong stench
From six feet under.

This human mouth is made not only
For eating food but also for talking trash.

The Air I Breathe

In this carnival of un-wellness
I have trekked miles
Of medical mines
Snaking in, slinking out between
Prostate, balloons, Tia's
MRI's, Plavix, Coumadin and aspirins
Now, angiograms in my veins
Stent troughs in my brain.
Only the spiritual universe
Knows when and how it will end.
The guinea pig scampering
To be well, blind as a post.
To see the inside of the human heart
Is the sign a Godly relief.
Lucky to still tell the world
And canonize the festivals
Of the unknowns.
I hope no angel or devil
Slates me on their calendars.
My mission is yet undone:
My family, my writing world.
Death has no assignment
With the air I breathe—
I hope.

David Levy
Neurosurgeon extraordinaire

A person from whose head
A louse is removed
Must be grateful.
A fowl does not forget where it lays its eggs.
The man who remembers others
Remembers his redeemer—the Osagyefo.

I came to you with corrosive
Dizzy spells—a stroke gathering storm
Like a temblor garnering implosion.
You took a risk, knowing
The weather could be rough
No venture, no gain.
The stroke, forthwith eloped.
It is not only the fox,
Even the snail arrives at its destination.

Now, I have a balloon in my head
To arrest my stenosis—
The narrowing of my
Middle left cerebral artery.
At the far away specialty—
Buffalo New York Hospital
Where other wizards gathered to vet their art on
Me—
The wizards who are no medical buffoons.

Without you, my noon
Could have turned an eclipse
And vegetated into nuclear mushroom
Oh, David:
Greatness and beauty
Do not belong to the gods alone.
They are yours.
Your excellence is the mustard seed of fame.
On a windy day,
It spreads far and wide.
One cannot wait
Till the evening hours
To pay gratitude

To one's guardian spirit,
When a ripe fruit
Sees an honest man,
It drops
I thank you beyond measure
For saving my life's breath.

Cerebral Angiogram

Hope is the unwillingness to die
When looking for health
In the ravens of ill-heath,
Where light seems
Incommodious to affect
The labyrinth maze of gullies
That accommodate nature's red ocean.

The doctors filled my maze
With their green ocean
Fishing for cerebral dykes
Or viscous debris that dam
The watershed of life.
My translucent corrosion
And blockage in my brain.
The thirsty fig stands patiently
Waiting for the arrival of the rain

The gods can only hear
One wish at a time—
My unwillingness to kick the bucket.
They must have heard my petitions,
Because a presence brought me to consciousness.
Still, as I awoke to life
I wondered, when the goat
Will be strong enough
To finally kill the leopard.

The Sea of Dry Vegetation

Sometimes—
Life is like the sea
Of dry vegetation,
The genesis is an oasis of fertility—
When thoughts and dreams are foundations
Of our beings.
We feel limitless and invincible
Hardwork, success and all.
Along the way,
Life throws us a strange curve.
We wonder what's amiss.
Criticism is easy
But does not create.
Only Yarabi* knows tomorrow.

Often, we humans forget
The calendar fate places on our heads.

Such is this blizzard of my life.
A time there was
When I was:
Chaka, the Zulu of my landscape
Ogedengbe Agbogungboro—the conqueror
Ifa, the Oracle of knowledge and profundity
Don Quixote of social miens
Mutesa, the King of Buganda
The Kabakayeka of history.

We are what we think makes us
But time sobers us all.
I hope the end is not near
I have learnt the great lessons of life
Ripe for my children to pluck.
A clay pot of water is never hot-tempered
Experience is the juice of time.

*Yarabi, God

Jay Rosenberg
The Moses

Caution be your name
Adamant and emphatic
"No surgery, please. A ticking time-bomb
the brain, the engine
of the mind,
Tinker with it,
 You bait death
And dare the devil.
Who knows
What the heart thinks?
There must be another way.
Levy and I agreed,
You will be fine"
If the heart carries life
It forgets death.

When the cock crows
It never stops again.
Once it matures
It warns the world
The times of decay.

Rosenberg, the town-crier
Rosenberg, the oracle
Rosenberg, the shaman
Rosenberg, the Moses:

I like the fuss over me
Someone is present when I sleep
Levy, a frontier's man
I hear you; I love you
Rosenberg, an eagle
Whose swoops have seen
Many seasons and floods
From the sky
What better contingent
Can a dog have?
The encyclopedia,
Speaks my language,
Heaven be praised.

Now That I Am Well

I carry the sun within me
My nights are lit with the full moon
Every new day the dawn inspires me
I hear the birds chirping in unison with the
Waterfalls
Nature's chorus of fidelity.

I spring briskly with my unseeing feet
My world fills with silence, the stillness of
Happiness.
My intimacy embraces distance from worries.
My heart works the miracles of the invincible.
I feel the presence of the unseen, and the
Hallelujah of resurrection

Who has not smelt death does not know the joy of
Living.
It is the warmth of the broken heart
The face does not stand the smoke
A firm tree does not bow to a storm
Ancestral spirits resist my demise
I wear the heart of the lion
A fitting tribute to my lineage.
Only dead fish swims
With the stream all the time.

My Epitaph — Whenever

Here sleeps the pretender:
Tayo Peter Olafioye,
Rehashing Death.
Never rich, never poor
Always true to the core.
A nonconformist anyway.
Tried but never was perfect.
Hoped so much
To be a scholar.
He who never tried
Is the one who failed.
A fish, he was
In many ponds of culture
In many a stream of civilization,
Some say: Colorful
But always an African at heart.

HARVEST SEASON

When our past caught up with the present and we began to reap the harvest of pains in our national delusion that we were smarter than those who went before. The feet of the corpse we buried yesterday began to show beneath the horrible mounds. We began to thrash around like atoms without cells. The feculence of our political rascalities deodarizes and nauseates the globe.

Book VI
The Parliament of Idiots
Tryst of Sinators

Dedication

To my troika of executive siblings whom I love very dearly, so that they may live forever in human consciousness.

Olu Olafioye
Of Obafemi Awolowo Foundation in Lagos. Retired Librarian of the National Library, Lagos.

Obafemi Olayeye
First cousin. A classicist.
Retired Principal, Teachers' College, Ode Aye.

Ademola Olayeye
Eldest of all. First cousin
Retired Assistant Director of Education, Ministry of Education, Lagos State.

Gratitude

Kunle Olafioye of Igbotako, Oshoro in Ikaleland; Tunde Lawal: Kwara Poly---Ilorin; and Tunde Asaju-Newswatch, Abuja; Jamie Anne Guerina, San Diego; for being my research assistants over the years.

A FILIAL APPRECIATION OF A MOTHER'S DEATH

These past few years constituted a turning point in my life. After forty, anything becomes possible. A cancer of the prostate, followed a few months later by a stroke, devastated me. I survived both with effective surgeries without chemotherapy or radiology. I remain a full man. Brain surgery with angioplasty stenting lifted the stroke threat. I am normal again. The account of these double whammy attacks within a few months gave birth to my narrative—*A Stroke of Hope*—that alerted the reading world what dying felt like. I also etched the work from my hospital bed as a legacy to bequeath my little girl – nine years old at the time—a document of what might have killed me, so that she might know what afflicted her father and how I might have passed on.

The strength of surviving these two serious visitations, my publishers and friends egged me to return home, to launch the six new works I managed to do at the time. I had left home eleven years before without a visceral reunion with my roots. Less fortunate candidates could have succumbed to any of these afflictions, so to live to tell about them deserved a festival of gratitude to my spiritual universe, ancestors, all the unseen and inexplicable entities. They knew why I endured and grew. My profound gratitude also extends to the American medical ingenuities and their providers. Without them, where would I have been?

I made the triumphant return home to raving reviews and acclaim. I could not have received a warmer welcome and appreciation. However, behind such ceremony, was lurking the next strange happening in my life. I have encountered many. My mother felt no joy when she saw me in Lagos. What came back home to her was not her vibrant son, the professor, who had left home some years before, but his ghost. Gaunt, scowlly, jowlly-jawed, emaciated, and dehydrated, a ripe candidate for expiration. I showed her the face of death, not mine. My countenance scared me too; a scarecrow, grimaced back at me from my pictures in the newspapers. All my families harried and feared the worst, especially my mother. Happily, however, Death does not visit all who lie sick-laden in bed.

139

I am her first-born. Telepathically, she concluded that I was going to die before her, given the gravity and ghoulish image. She became quietly determined that such an unnatural tragedy would not happen in her lifetime. She refused to plant her adult son in the grave before her time. I could read the fright in her eyes, as she complained bitterly daily about my comatose kinetic dynamics.

She was living her retirement years with my sister in Lagos. My condition formed their menu of daily conversations. Days before my return to the United States, I paid her my last visit. We enjoyed a good time of warm and hearty family chats. I never suspected this closeness knowing that it would be the last.

After some hours, I stood to take my leave. My mother and sister walked me to the front yard. Strangely, my mother chose not to look at me as we walked to the car. Transfixed, she looked at the ground at her feet. She screwed up her face into a determined grimace. My heart thundered, telling me that my mother was going through a transformation. She did not wave a goodbye. She did not look up. She did not say a word. She did not move an inch until my car diminished out of her sight. For that symbolic omen, I knew that an ominous stoke was going to mark me before the year 2000, ran out. The blow did not take long. Three weeks after I returned to America, the phone rang in the dark to wake me up in San Diego. The weeping voice of my younger brother from London announced: "Mother died this morning, 6 A.M. Lagos time." Possibly, my mother died of old age, of natural causes, but the circumstance of her death lent itself to cultural interpretations.

I felt a bolt strike me from the depth of my being. I knew right away, metaphysically, that my mother had died my death. She had willed herself to die. She had called to herself a death of self-sacrifice. My sister reported to me where my mother chose to be buried . She had not sickened, she did not suffer, even a cold or fever. On the eve of her death, she had asked my sister to pray for her. She went to bed. At 5 A.M., she woke my sister up to ask her for a bath. My sister gave her one. That was my mother's last ritual. At 6 A.M., she lay dead. For now, only absence connects between us.

Most of the western world may not understand or believe that cultural deaths exist, metaphysical deaths. We Africans paint life with cultural artifacts, the cosmos of spirits, totems, national struggles and accepted beliefs, most of which best transmit the African writer's message because of familiarity or well-known imagistic references and assimilation. We are still rich in virgin happenings to write about, not daffodils or Mt. Rushmore, or the mighty Mississippi or the legacy of the Nazis. For the most part, Western literary conceptions no longer have such ethnic resources any more to rely upon. They revel in the post-modern modernist literary consciousness. They dwell in the new worlds of intertextualities, computers, Internet, astrophysics, cinematography, space exploration and the like, as their environments alert them. What serious African writer would want to imitate any western style of writing, good or bad? We float in the world of virgin materials that best inform our creativity. They flounder in the world of cosmetics. We swim in the world of pristine spirits and metaphysics; theirs bear no names. What they say or think little matters. The African chronicler must stay true to his environment to remain relevant. He must breathe typically African atmospheres while he reaches out to touch the universal. He cannot afford to commit a cultural incest or to lock himself into a refrigerator; he must maintain a measure of cultural and environmental affinity and fidelity.

In my Yoruba cultural totem, a mother's life conclusion is successful when her children outlive her to perform funeral obsequies over her. In death a mother or father wears richly ornamented traditional clothing, hand woven in the heirloom. Through this particular fabric of red and purple outlay, is an Alaari: A proverbial profundity weaves: "My child, when I pass on, please drape me with an Alaari outfit." This choice of cloth carries a cultural significance. This traditional flag of recognition and of life's success up-drapes a parent. My mother wanted that rite and I am pleased that she received her earned reward. As our culture recognizes it, a parent to whom his or her children give a fitting burial, wears the mantle of a successful parenthood.

I am also pleased that she died a decent death: no prolonged illness, not even for a day. I am glad that she last saw me. That remained her wish, one that always marked the last paragraph in her letters, "to see you again before I answer the call of my fathers." My mother died the death of honor, a sacrificial death. She did not want to witness the death of her grown child, not only a nightmarish tragedy but also a cultural disgrace, a cultural taboo. This disgrace, an "ofo," an utmost cultural tragedy, imposes itself upon her as she understood and accepted the label. Unimaginable, this burden looms psychologically perilous to lift. I am well again incidentally, bouncy and alive. My mother died for me. With her spiritual tunnel vision, she will watch over my siblings and me. I so pray and believe.

Today, I mourn the death of my two mothers: my biological mother Elizabeth Kehinde, and my natal mother, Nigeria, a motherland to which my heart belongs. Then when I was visiting my natural mother, the death or dishonor and besmirching of my natal mother, Nigeria, doubly ravaged my heart. The probe of the senate leaders and the impeachment that ensued exposed the betrayal of polity which meant the asphyxiation of this young democracy, my motherland, my Nigeria. This primal land gave birth to us, and many of us own no other to which we intuitively belong. To see her through this deathly elder- abuse at the hands of a few prodigal sons and daughters, gave me the creeps, the scars of the heart and a thorned, smashed soul. These thankless children drank up her honey of dreams and milk of societal regeneration, through financial irregularities and deep-seated insensitivity. Not only these are to blame but also, those who pretentiously and facetiously put up stances of innocence.

Such elegiac musings that bled the heart of this poet gave rise to the chronicling of these narrative monodies and threnodies: The Parliament of Idiots: Tryst of the Sinators.

San Diego, California
2001

I. The Sky Can't Keep Its Secrets

One Day

One day I'll sail the troubled seas
using my heart as a compass.

Someday I'll rid the world of AIDS
using my songs as a prescription.

Someday I'll raid the governance of stench
using my poems as bombs.

Someday I'll wipe the world of leprosy
using my art of poetry.

Someday I'll slaughter the whales of diseases
using my pens as harpoons.

Someday I'll poach tribalism called racism
using my works as arrows.

Someday I'll forge a true nation
using my umbrella of the rainbow.

One day I'll unite the world
using the language of humanity

United Nations Headquarters
New York, New York

The Conclave of Hyenas

They sheared the elephant*:
arms, legs, and limbs
flesh, carcass, and tusks.
Its heart gulped in a flash
the foxes provided for themselves
and over gorged their esophagus
like dogs they barked backwards
not seeing their fronts.
They played the lions,
and wildebeests without tails.
These tribal hyenas—
the G5: Lagido*, Heirat
Adan, Ikoko*and Ikeregbe*—
laid the royal bed
that cushioned Ogidan's bones
they were the chambermaids of horror
in the hierarchy of poli-prostitution
the contract scam:
a festival of smut from above
all germinated
the murk subconscious
the odor of the skunk
followed their trails

Once aliens devastated our shores
their bones lay in our soil
formed the rivers of ashes underneath.
Now, the internal antagonists
are the locusts that ruin the crops.
They mat the acreage with their underbellies
they too will die from the heat of the earth.

Non-intended corporations
siphoned away thousand millions:
Cee Chris, Centre & Point, Asso Logistics
all a ruse in technocracy
many checks posted mystically in accounts
contracts approved without process
where possible, they signed with their toes
laptops by Tritech Computers
without limit like bonuses without merit.

One should not acquire more
when sharing ill-gotten inheritance.
That the cat can climb and dismount
make him fall into a ditch.

These idiots really tested the stone
to see if it bled water.
Now they know
Niger stones shed tears and blood.
Any ventriloquist could have
read such a future for their hopes
no conscience, no logic
no democratic temper—
their peoples already comatose
compliment of Abacha's vitrol,
the totalitarian mammon
whose people, daily like cats,
eat stone breads for dinner
Voltore, Voltore all,
on the rooftops of our domiciles.

For as long as we have memories
Yesterday shall remain unforgotten.

Lagos

*Elephant, Nigerian national treasury or resources
*Lagido, monkey
*Ikoko, wolf
*Ikeregbe, the goat

Crows of the Roach

Ikeregbe's* spittoon
Gave his superiors waves of the brain
Farted lots of putrid
A constantly decaying sludge
His tumor ferments
Puked, at the probe, scams
Never before diagnosed
The landscape drenched in red slush
And blood stained debris
No formaldehyde can
Neutralize the stench.

He sank miles deep
Into the ethical swamp
In this season of political vertigos
Like the eagle above, he forgot to realize
Those below were watching him
Other critters then mooed
They did not understand
The language of deceit
Should not have feared
The heat of the sun
Truth would have blunted
Its intensity.

The he-goat was once a cattle egret
But now, a roach,
Knows no stream of action to swim
But the drools of the mouth
Now he does not know
Where he lost his memory
He that swallows the mortar
Shall forever remain uncomfortable.

The goat bleats in the pen
No one knows why till now
Since grief has no credentials.

*Ikeregbe, The Stubborn Goat, goofy and erratic

147

The cock that had crowed
Olumo to Aso rock,
Had failed all with
Inadequacy and incompetence
Hence the dyke broke loose.
Every one carved a territory
To dismember the unity.
Our hope is a bird in flight.

Lagos, Nigeria

OGIDAN—The Mountain Lion

His only flaw—
A scholastic naivety—
Usually the bane of swots
As always, he stirred
The calm trees
Forgetting that no creature
Can stay still
In a tornado of lightning.
Imperially slim and nobly endowed,
He glittered when he walked
Elegantly impeccable with a tail whisk
Chiefly accosted, the Oyi—
Humorously human when he testified,
Brilliant like a fox
Who condemns the trap
But not himself.
A mule
Courted by incapacity
For imagination.

His face has felt
The harmattan* howls
When he hid to set a fire
He forgot that
He could not hide the smoke.

The black Mamba, the old whip in the forest
Waited to maul the stray dog
Corruption without end-
The old Mamba had two birth certificates
Each a different date and name
Three grammar schools
None which he attended
Even the British Middle Temple
A claim, a cloud, then a tussle.
At this crossroads,
An egg, a kernel and a stone.
Under the Olumo, a hybrid
Of snakes and tortoises

*Harmattan - African cold, dry wind that usually blows from the Sahara desert
from December to March

Ogidan let down the sharp knife of his mind
Allowing the massacres in the Savannah
The eagle did not know
What was in the pit

Ogidan once plastered ancestral pillars,
Awo and Zik, with his tongue.
Now he muzzled the Sinate
With brain and abracadabra
Swallowing the decibels of self importance
While nemeses were digging trenches
Under his dome
Contracts flowed the recipes of distort
Like floods through his unsuspecting dykes
I felt his funeral in my heart.

He advertised his brilliance
On the billboards of illusion.
However wise the young,
He cannot be richer
Than the aged in experience.
When delirious with certainty
He forgot the wraths of the departed.
And swelled like an interior sun
In his sugar of vanity
He was oblivious
Of the tortoises under the rock
They concorted honeys of untruths;
By accident as usually happens
They put a political plug
Through his gullet
A probe, an impeachment,
Their irrational exuberance
Our sullen art of mismanagement
Those who killed the domestic animal
Are not our heroes

The curse of the aged
If it dims in the morn
Will assure a hit in the twilight.
The Oyi who stylishly robed
Fell like the waterfall in the Sun
His effort from the beginning
Was the condemnation of fate—

The Emperor has no clothes.
Others: irrational warriors
Of terror.

San Diego, California

Azikiwe's Curse

It was from the tongue of Edoni*
That the hyena earned
The curse of irrationality:
Always youthful and strong but intemperate
His volcanic bursts:
The language of mental dysfunction
If we fish intensely
We would find a crippled fish.
Any repair, too late
Do not tangle with the spirits
Only an oracle could dance
To their drums.

Schiphol International Airport
Amsterdam, Holland

*Edoni-a 13th century Benin Monarch

The Impeachment

"Ogidan impeached"
The papers blared
The elephant has fallen
The king ditched in the abyss
Obalufon* blinked in outrage
Lightning struck in the forest
Bonfires leveled the savannah.
Kipling once said:
"Fame and disaster come
One after the other
Treat them the same, my son."

This has long been coming
When detractors spat his name
As the tobacco phlegm of disgust.
His brinkmanship at large
Earned him the curse of their pains
Actually, the monarch
Started to fall
From the hour of coronation
So mazed their web of unforgiveness
Only because he wore the cap
Of the sage and the parrot's.
You do not undermine those
Whose maneuvers are
As impure as your own.
They denied him the twilight of existence.

Once giddy with power and illusion
Commandeered the national mace
His staff of office
But the property of the nation
Hid it in his village
To douse the embers of plots
To ditch him; they never quit, those
Witches and wizards of pursuit
When will the goat not be sacrificed?
Time will tell and it did
Adroitly played the chess of survival
Used lofty gibbers

*Obalufon - An Ife supreme legendary monarch

153

To confuse and contuse
The erudition of the press
And his peers in the Sinate.
The home plate like the calabash
Of the pantheons,
Is never known to be wholly clean,
The woods would avenge themselves

When life is rather giddy
One should be careful
No one's love abides
Except that of one's own destiny
Political humpiness or marriage
Never Lasts
Too many ghosts lurking
Behind the bridal suite.

And then, it happened:
The Niger cyclones of sand
The inimical elements that stifle
And blindfolds without regards—
Those who are too smart
Often become victims
Of their own cleverness
Malfeasance, the abuse of office and scams
They charged—
Roasting and decapitating the elephant.
Who is afraid of the Oyi?
Those whose thrones he rattles
—Tornadic force—
Before or in 2003

Awards to selves and cronies
Irregularities in accounts
Unregistered bedfellows, mostly ghosts
Precipitate contract awards without clearance
Signed evidence undeniable
It was the fleecing of the forest
National treasury thus debauched
National projects prodigalized
National assets prostituted
National spirits assassinated—
Crimes against humanity and the dispossessed
Be careful though—the rat-finks

Who wear calico shrouds of falsehood.

This child—democracy—
Or Osundare's 'demoncrazy'
Too fragile at this time,
To toss so flippantly
Needs cultural menus of nurture.
The past is a pain-fest
Too fresh to forget
Measures must be taken, ostensibly,
To dam up the flood
Hence the impeachment
Of Ogidan and fellow prostitutes
81 to 11 vote
73%: two–thirds of 109
Nobody says:
The lynchers are stainless
Like the calico or linen

Florie's florid of tears
The last to walk the Emperor
Out of office and grace
Oh! The heaviness of poli-machinations,
The Macbeths and Brutus of Africa.

When you were sober with brilliance
If all the hairs on our heads
        Were tongues,
They would not have sung enough
        Of your praise in honey-flavored tunes.

Ikoyi, Lagos

Credentials

Some of those
Certified to legislate our lives
Have none of their own
The ethical swamp at the equiator
How do you get diamond or gold
In the midst of rot?
The whole foundation a festering sore
A nation where magpies
Are kings.
Please remove them.
They over reach
Their inadequacy.

Agege, Lagos State

News-Channel 10

Let us revise the past
To learn from it—
We hope.
Abacha regime and the like
Their national voice—NTA lies
The unabashed authority of manipulation
Who trumpet the dictionary of distorts
Their index of fictions:
The government was immaculate
Its veins, quite transparent
The economy, very buoyant
The Head of State, simply strident
Until the coup of God struck
When he least expected.
That medium with a leprous tongue
A jaundiced crocodilian Cyclops
Does not know
Where it left its memory
For truth and decency.
Sanni was:
The solitary Commander of Dynamism
The very soul of Eternity
Cardiac arrest however nipped him
On the theater of libidinous activity
In a hotel at night
Now that he was forced to hell
The nation was reborn
NTA shines a renaissance
And many other siblings breathe on their own
To aid the farm of progress
The God of Justice never slept.

NTA-Nigerian Television Authority
Ikoyi-Lagos

Prisoners of History

We are all prisoners of history
Only truth and reconciliation:
Our retrieval.

You won't know,
Where you are going
Until you know
Where you have been.

Exposing the truth
Goes to the heart of issues.

The truth of the past,
However ugly,
    Heals the future.

What are we about?

Crimes against humanity:

Epical slavery in diaspora
Holocaust in Hitlerism, 6 million roasted
Apartheid of South Africa, a people's denigration
Pol pot, the million skulls of Cambodia
The Philippines—never to forget Japan
Korea, the sex slaves of the Emperor
Internments: the "Japs" in America
Yankee slaves in Asia
Polish Jews—the 16,000 massacres
To whom the Pope apologized not long ago
20 million Russians—
Stalin and Hitler sacrificed
The ethnic cleansings of Kosovo
Alabanians, dispossessed and dislodged
Birmingham bombers of hate, 1963
4 black girls and the House of God pulverized

Jews and gentiles of Biblical
Proportions in Egypt
Just a tip of the iceberg
Vatican, the Janus
Always looking away

Even today
Some of the past still remains
Conscience always shattered
By events of the past.

Who will atone?

My son,
Confession and acknowledgement first
Then, forgiveness:
The only suitable exchange
For our lost humanity.
Without forgiveness
There is no future
Though nothing can ever
Compensate Pain.
Admission is our feel-good tonic
Twin sister of therapy and apology.
We deceive ourselves
If we think we know who we are
Without it.
Someone must atone
    And
Someone will accept and appreciate
Truth alone is no substitute for justice
But reconciliation is
Our self retrieval.
Events do not often die a permanent death
They relive across generations
Faulkner says:
History is not what was but is
    And
Whoever accuses all humanity
Can only find one guilty.
Without forgiveness
There is no tomorrow
Though some long ago deeds,
Deserve punishment
That we may never forget
Moving on we must
As the earth around the sun,
    Oh, Copernicus

Johannesburg, South Africa

The Disobedient Fowl

Only God says, "I am"
And He is
Only God boasts, "It is me"
And it is
Not Chube Ogidan.
The Ogbuefi* of his State
Boasts to defend him
A N200 million kitty.
The bravado
The bravura
The bold face
The chest beating
All a package of fallacy named corruption
A game face in spite of the obvious
The micro-dot place, the failure chain
Of Ogidan in history
Now that he is impeached—
However mischievously.
A mess in the Savannah
But an intransigent fowl
Obeys willy-nilly in the pot of soup.

Ilorin, Kwara State

VII
The Fish Rots from the Head

The Garden of Dreams

Flowers tinged with colors
red, white, purple or green
like a barren woman
who dances with a baby
in her dreams.
For some, when lightening strikes
rain never follows
to make rich their green.
Never grows lushness
to make fresh their smell.
Hangs dry in the air
like a palace of emptiness or aridity,
a horticulture composition of thorns.
The Garden of Eden,
metaphor for discomfort or blessings
where dreams grow true, sometimes
through the dints of labor.
Giddy thrusts do not make wealth
only work, luck, or timing.
A peanut pod serves
 a drink to fill, for some.
Others acquire,
the dictionary of distort
successive failures
or manipulations
where morality receives no acknowledgement
just walks out of the door.
The garden of dreams
hangs in the parlor of imagination
or the landscape of unfulfillment.
The garden of dreams can spell
the ministry of sorrow
where flowers like youths
do not reach their full life.
They whither in the boulevards
of existence and expectancy—
Cenotaphs of remembrance,
in family sorrows,
looking at the wounds of yesterday.
Even a nation
can pile a sad history

of its experience.

Amsterdam, Holland
29 June 2000

Godlinitis

My family and nation suffer Godlinitis
that is:
an acute attack of Godliness
very painful to watch
almost moronic slavery
stretching God to the extreme
he never decreed.
Excess in professing
excess in tithing
the sacrifice of needs
to salivate Heavenliness
while the proclaimed messengers live it up
on earth: The sleek cars
latest clothings, psycho-semantic
Oratories, catchy phrases
of devotional surrealism
indoctrination and occasional mental coitus
this Pentecostal madness,
with a two drink minimum and
a rim shot to follow.

Also in Africa
same hero-worshipping of cultic proportions
crowning spiritual fathers
who are always
dandy, dainty and decorated
looking chic in spiritual splendor,
cultural outfits and rosy cheeks—
compliments of the women—
their weekly multi-dollar contributions
paid like a bill
monetary obligation
to the church-goers' invisible hero
their own natal needs defy
scriptural prescriptions.
an insanity of biblic proportions
this worship:
to me, an emotional idiocy.
the country oscillates the pendulums
despite the spiritual passions, why?
Dishonesty my friends

something onery and amiss
to crave spirituality, morn, noon and night
vociferous prayer attitudinizing
frenetic and passionate tongue-speaking:
Indian mantras really, twin sisters: of
unintelligible gibbers and dramatic ecstasy.
not wrong to be Godly
but practice with credulity
and manageable reality
not mad-cow fanaticism.
Only God knows
those who worship Him.
mindless money pursing dodos-
without church members
they cannot survive
the irony of these Heavenly chameleons.

When her majesty rails at home
I never see or feel or know
Jesus Christ on her tongue.
only:
showiness and sassiness
the true sheep of the Lord.
But:
character, my only catechism of Godliness.

San Diego, California
6 August 2000

Talking Responsibility

The owl is wisest of all birds
The more it sees,
The less it talks.
It's called maturity
But in self defense the parrot
Makes a talkative.

La Jolla, California, USA
5 September 2000

The Music of My Heart

Let me be the sun that warms your night
Let me be the tunes that caress your happiness
Let me be the air that freshens your lungs
Le me be the spring that cleans your veins
Let me be the flower that seasons your beauty
Let me be the bulwark on which you lean
Let me be the roof that shields your worries
Let me be the home in which you live
Let me be the anchor on which you berth
Let me be your songs the polyphonies of rarity
Let me, let me, let me
Be the meeting point of our two circles—
    The universe of our oneness!

Lagos, Nigeria
5 August 2000

I Will Love You

Till night becomes day
Ghana becomes Zimbabwe
A river swallows the sea
An ocean covers the mountain
The dolphin sings in the alley
The wall grows an ear
The world becomes flat
And the elephant dances the Marumba

I will love you
Till flowers smile at night
Months run like cheetahs
The stars drink the rain
Eternity moves without motion
The Pacific turns a Sahara
Disorder becomes my order
Nothing matters anymore
Only the harmony of your heart.

Los Angeles, California
8 June 2001

Amadou Diallo of Senegal

Oh, Jibulu
My ancestor,
I tremble
With my heart in my throat
This atrocity impales our race
They killed Amadou Diallo
A Wollof of Senegal in New York
Where the heart of America,
Is a deep Freeze.

This confrontation
A racial marginality
The only way home
Only through memories
The past and present
We are the cattle fodders
For the beasts of intolerance.

Forty-one bullets
Into an African of 22
Without provocation
Mowed down
Like a blade of grass
How many bullets
Does one need to die?

We are the history
Of our experience
Animals of sacrifice.
For how long O Eternity
Shall we pay for this paint?
An evil trade in misery
Kill one, kill all
Four police executioners!
The stars are watching
For we have a long historical memory
The burden of this shade
No species lives such an incineration.

"I don't understand
what happen to my son,"
the mother wailed
When will the goat be strong
To tame this leopard.

New York City
25 June 2000

Nature

There sits
A mountain of grief
In my heart,
When I browse the terrains
Of the human condition
On the Internet of postulation
These troubled lands:
India and Pakistan
Their nuclear fuse and harassments
Only a flicker or clicker—
The Armageddon of mutual destruct.
The nature's anger from the deep
Earthquake reshapes
California, Iran, Russia, Peru, and Japan
    Of course,
Nature's fury from the sky
Tornadoes and hurricanes—
Their ugly mascaras disfigure
Florida and the Caribbean
    Then Follows,
Nature's punishment of torrid flows
Europe, Mozambique, Nicaragua, California:
So many lives flushed.
    Above all,
The human nature of the mind
Need I say it—war,
Over a hundred of them at a time—Afghanistan,
Iraq, Chechnya, Angola, Kosovo, Sierra Leone
Some people
Surcharge insanity
For the polyphemus carnage.
Humans will never have peace
Their flailing tongues are the snakes.